The Story Behind Asia's Largest Animal Welfare Shelter

With 108 Photos

Glen Johnson

and Gary Johnson

www.soidog.org

For –

Margot Homburg

and

John & Gill Dalley

who have made everything
possible by following their hearts.

And to all the contributors and
volunteers who makes Soi Dog possible.

.

CONTENTS

SOI DOG

The Winner of the Great Nonprofit Award for three years running.

"May all that have life be delivered from suffering."

Buddha

"The greatness of a nation and its moral progress can be judged by the way its animals are treated."

Mahatma Gandhi

Throughout the book there are web-addresses that will direct you to the corresponding webpage.

© A puppy in the Puppy Run at Soi Dog.

Hello, I am the author Glen Johnson, and I (along with my brother Gary) will be taking you on the Soi Dog tour. We spent two months at the foundation (May and June. Then August and September 2015), chatting with the volunteers, the staff, and John and Gill Dalley – the co-founders, and generally getting the feel of the whole operation, as well as going out and experiencing catching the stray dogs firsthand, and taking a tour of the facility, as well as volunteering at the foundation, so we can convey their story to you.

Also, this book wouldn't be possible without the help of everyone at Soi Dog. I would especially like to say thank you to: John and Gill Dalley, Martin Turner, Paul Lloyd, Diana Van De Wall, Inga Annika, Darren Benbrook, and Pond Akkarin.

Glen Johnson
(September 2015)

1

THE SOI DOG FOUNDATION

© Gill Dalley – one of the co-founders.

Soi Dog's was created to improve the welfare of dogs and cats in Thailand. To better the lives for both the animal and human communities, and to end animal cruelty, and to ultimately create a society without homeless animals.

This is their aim.

This is their dream.

This is what they are striving to achieve with your help.

Soi Dog is a not-for-profit, legally registered charitable organization in Thailand, the United States, Australia, the UK, France, and Holland.

Soi Dog helps the homeless, neglected and abused dogs and cats of Thailand. They tirelessly work to end the dog meat trade throughout the region, and responds to animal welfare disasters and emergencies. They aim to set an example for the Asian region on how to humanely reduce the number of unwanted dogs and cats through spaying and neutering, and to better the lives and living conditions of the stray dogs and feral cats of Asia.

De-sexing (sterilization) has been proven to be the most effective way to help the animals. Soi Dog has reached a milestone of eighty-two thousand dogs and cats sterilized (to date).

Thousands more have been treated for injury and disease by providing emergency and ongoing veterinary treatment for abused and neglected street dogs and cats.

Soi Dog runs a shelter and rehoming center for over four hundred dogs (at present that's growing daily) that have been abandoned or abused and subjected to sometimes terrible cruelty.

They also feed hundreds of dogs and cats who live in temples around the large island of Phuket (where the foundation is located), and those that have been rescued from the dog meat trade.

They also help place rescued dogs and cats in caring homes all around the world.

Soi means alley in Thai. A fitting name, helping animals whose home is now the back streets of the cities, towns, and villages.

This book will give you an overview of the whole organization, and what they are striving to achieve and what they have achieved to date.

You will learn everything there is to know about Soi Dog, and the people who spend their lives helping the neglected dogs and cats of Thailand. People who have suffered immense personal injury in the pursuit of protecting the animals that have no voice, and who need someone to stand up for them.

You will meet the people who make Soi possible, who volunteer their time and energy into the foundation. People who have drastically changed his or her life in order to make a difference. You will read their stories and those of the animals that have been saved.

Welcome to the Soi Dog Foundation, Asia's largest animal welfare shelter.

2

AN INTRODUCTION TO SOI DOG

The Soi Dog Foundation as it is today was established in Phuket during 2003 by Dutch national Margot Homburg, and a British couple, John and Gill Dalley. Appalled by the tragic plight of the island's fifty thousand street dogs and cats, and the fact that no-one was doing anything about improving the situation; the trio decided the most sustainable solution to ending the misery of the animals was a mass vaccination and sterilization programme, giving medical access to those animals that needed it. Their efforts would have little impact in the short term, but the long-term vision was to make the island of Phuket a street dog and cat-free zone; therefore, a place where street dogs and cats would no longer suffer lives of misery, hunger, sickness, pain, and rejection.

The operation started as a single mobile sterilization unit on the island. Specific locations would be chosen based on density of street dogs and cats, and every morning the team would set up stall. Margot, John, and Gill acted as the animal welfare officers, whilst overseas volunteer vets and vet's assistants would perform the surgery. Several local vets also carried out sterilization operations for Soi Dog, at cost price.

During this initial period of the Soi Dog operations, the team came across many cases of sick and injured animals. Lacking facilities and manpower to treat them, the team would take the animals to a local vet and pay for the costs themselves.

The same scenario continued up until October 2004, when Gill suffered a horrendous personal tragedy, losing both legs after contracting an infection when saving a drowning dog. However, at Gill's insistence, the mobile clinic continued to operate throughout her recuperation period.

The tsunami that struck south-east Asia on Boxing Day 2004 hit the region particularly badly, with tens of thousands of people killed.

As well as affecting humans, thousands of dogs and cats were displaced, so Soi Dog focused on rescuing and treating as many of them as possible. The high profile coverage Phuket received throughout the world as a result of the tsunami attracted an influx of overseas volunteer vets and vet's nurses wanting to help. This meant that Soi Dog was sometimes able to run two or three mobile clinics simultaneously throughout the region.

A few months after the tsunami, Soi Dog received a two-year grant from WSPA, which helped the foundation fund its first clinic at a rented building in the capital of Phuket, with two vets and some support staff. This gave Soi Dog the ability to treat most of the sick and injured animals it came across in the course of its mobile sterilization programme. Despite the clinic not being a shelter, at one stage Soi Dog homed almost a hundred dogs and cats there. However, the conditions were not ideal, and in spring 2006 the foundation was offered the chance to use a government-owned dog pound in the north of the island.

Severely lacking even the most basic of facilities, Soi Dog invested three million baht (almost ninety thousand dollars) to bring the shelter up to an acceptable level, which included the installation of a basic clinic.

However, soon after all the improvements were completed, the government served notice to Soi Dog to leave the pound, stating that non-government organizations should not be responsible for running government facilities – even though they were the ones that offered it to them in the first place.

This led to a search for other premises, and in 2008 Soi Dog found some land for rent with outbuildings in the north of the island at Mai Khao. Work then begun to develop the site into a proper shelter and clinic, capable of holding up to four hundred dogs at any time. The charity now owns all the land the shelter is built on, and in late 2014 began constructing a new state-of-the-art dog hospital on site.

2011 saw two big challenges for Soi Dog. Firstly, a

distemper outbreak in Phuket that affected thousands of dogs. Thanks to the generosity of Soi Dog
supporters, the outbreak was quickly contained.
During the third quarter of 2011, heavy, prolonged
flooding in central Thailand caused the displace-
ment of thousands of dogs and cats. Together with a
number of other animal welfare charities such as
Wildlife Friends of Thailand, Soi Dog set up operations to rescue and treat these animals – funded by
generous donations from supporters.

2011 also saw the start of the Trade of Shame
campaign, designed to stop the illegal trade in dogs
for consumption from Thailand to Vietnam and
China. By March 2015, there had been well over a
hundred arrests of smugglers, butchers, and tannery
owners, compared with only two in the whole of the
previous fifteen years.

In 2012, a silver lining emerged from the dark
cloud of the 2011 central Thailand flooding, with Soi
Dog's decision to open a treatment clinic in Bangkok,
for the estimated six hundred thousand street dogs
and cats there. The major focus of the new operation
was to conduct a mass sterilization and vaccination
programme across the city, which will take a good
few years to complete. The clinic also treats animals
in need of medical attention.

Also in 2012, with support from Dogs Trust
International, the Prevent Unwanted Puppies (PUP)
programme commenced in Phuket. This saw the
number of sterilization operations rise to just under
twenty-thousand per year by 2014. By March 2015,
over eighty percent of the street dogs and cat
population had been sterilized, meaning the popul-

ation was officially "under control."

From a very small operation back in 2003, Soi Dog has grown over the year's thanks to donations from core loyal supporters who share the foundation's vision.

Today, around sixty people work for or volunteer at the charity in both Phuket and Bangkok, including local vets and vet's assistants, local animal welfare officers, Burmese shelter staff, volunteer dog walkers, dog socialisers, volunteer tour guides, and volunteer office staff.

Soi Dog receives no government funding, and is entirely reliant on donations from members of the public.

Today, Soi Dog's operations in Phuket covers five main interrelated fields:

1. Sterilization and vaccination of street dogs and cats.

2. Medical treatment for the sick and injured.

3. Sheltering.

4. Adoption.

5. Public (schools) education on animal welfare issues.

As of July 2015 over eighty-eight thousand dogs and cats had been sterilized, meaning a critical mass of over eighty percent of the stray population cannot reproduce. This is statistically significant; it means the stray population is rapidly declining. Soon Phuket will be home to a much smaller, healthier, sustainable dog population.

The next major sterilization and vaccination project (as already stated) for Soi Dog will be in Bangkok, home to over six hundred thousand street dogs and cats. The programme is expected to take between seven and ten years to complete.

In 2013, Soi Dog was instrumental in forming the Asia Canine Protection Alliance (ACPA) with Animals Asia, Change for Animals Foundation and Humane Society International. The dual objectives of this alliance are to work with the respective governments of Cambodia, Laos, Thailand, and Vietnam to eliminate rabies, and to end the dog and cat meat trades in these countries.

3

JOHN AND GILL DALLEY'S STORY

On the surface, John and Gill Dalley seemed like any other British couple retiring to Phuket in Thailand. Both having had successful careers in England, Gill as a banker, and John in the chemicals industry, it was time to take things easy. After years of the 9 to 5 routine, they were ready to make a radical change in lifestyle and give something back to society.

The couple had married in Phuket in 1996, and instantly fell in love with the paradise island on the West Coast of Thailand. They returned on many occasions after their wedding for holidays, and had decided early on that when they did have enough money to retire, Phuket would become their final home.

In 2003, their dream came true. With pensions assured, they sold up in Leeds, West Yorkshire, and flew to Phuket to start their new lives. John was fifty-three and Gill was forty-four.

Gill and John had no intention of living a sedentary lifestyle in Thailand. Both wanted to help out in the local Phuket community as a way of giving something back to the island that had left them with so many happy memories over the years. John had already pre-determined that he wanted to do something about the stray dog and cat problem on the island, which, in reality, was not limited to Phuket; it was, and continues to be, a major issue across the whole of the country.

On previous trips to the island, the Dalley's had noticed not just the sheer number of stray dogs and cats living on the streets (an estimated fifty thousand at the time), but the appalling condition of most of them.

As John said, "We were a bit shocked at first. Most of the dogs were emaciated through malnutrition. Many had mange and were covered in sores. Some had open wounds, which could have been caused by road traffic accidents, dog fights or human cruelty. Many of the wounds were infested with parasites and maggots, and riddled with infection. They were living on the streets without anyone to care for them. I wanted to find a solution to improve their lives, but was unsure how to do this. The scale of the problem was just so overwhelming."

Gill meanwhile had planned to teach English to under-privileged children, but this proved difficult as there were already so many people doing this. So instead, Gill made the decision to work with John on addressing the street dog and cat problem.

© John feeding street dogs at a temple in Phuket.

Gill stated, "You couldn't walk ten yards down a street without seeing a dog in the most terrible, terrible conditions."

As they set about investigating what was already being done to help the street dogs and cats, they met a lady called Margot Homburg, a Dutch expatriate who had also just moved to Phuket (from Bangkok). She had been sterilizing dogs in her local neighborhood in Bangkok by taking them to a local vet, and had set up a charity called Soi Dog Foundation. They joined forces, and decided that the best long-term solution to the street dog and cat problem in Phuket was mass sterilization. This would not have any effect in the short-term, but in the long run it would significantly reduce the number of animals being born on the streets to suffer a life of misery, hunger, pain, and rejection.

Their ambitious plan was to run a mobile sterilization clinic across the island.

John, Gill, and Margot became the animal welfare officers (and occasionally the vet's assistants), whilst the sterilization operations themselves were carried out by overseas volunteer vets and nurses. An Australian vet who had been running a small-scale sterilization programme focusing on the numerous temples in Phuket, where many stray dogs are taken in by the monks, passed on her equipment to Soi Dog when she moved to Hong Kong.

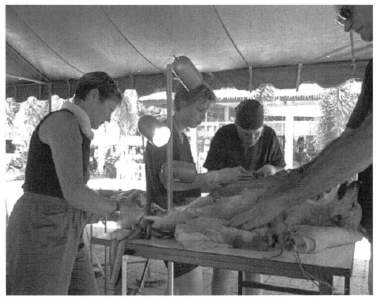

© One of Soi Dog's first mobile sterilization clinic operations, 2003.

Two local vets also offered their sterilization services at cost price, so the programme began as a very small but effective and well thought-out operation.

At this stage, Soi Dog had no facilities to treat injured or diseased animals they found on the streets; neither did they have the facilities to shelter the animals until they completed their rehabilitation. Basic medical care was administered on the spot, but if the animal needed specialist treatment, John, Gill and Margot would take the animals to a local vet and pay for the treatment themselves. This was not a sustainable solution however, because they were living on a limited pension income.

4

PERSONAL TRAGEDY STRIKES GILL

In September 2004, disaster struck.

The group were running a mobile sterilization clinic in a small village close to where they lived. As already stated, John, Gill and Margot were essentially the animal welfare officers and vet's assistants.

Gill went to a nearby builder's merchant where she had seen several street dogs.

One large dog looked aggressive and unfriendly, so she decided it would require blow darting.

Gill states, "Dogs that we can't pick up easily, we chemically blow dart them with an anesthetic."

However, having darted it the dog raced off into a flooded water buffalo field before the dart had taken effect. The water was about eighteen inches high. Knowing that the dog would most likely drown once the tranquilizer kicked in, and the animal sunk below the dirty water, Gill quickly started wading through the sodden field and eventually managed to retrieve the semiconscious animal. As Gill reached the dog, it was just starting to collapse below the waterline. The dog was large, and she struggled to drag the unconscious animal hundreds of meters through the flooded field to dry ground, unaware that while she was in the water, bacteria was seeping into her bloodstream that would change her life forever.

"When I got to her, she was just starting to go down under the water," Gill says. "I got to her just in time, and I kind of half dragged her under the armpits back to the road."

A few days later, Gill began to feel seriously ill, and complained of terrible pain in her legs. She knew something was seriously wrong and asked John to take her to the hospital.

John rushed her to a local hospital, and she was immediately admitted to the intensive care unit.

Gill stated that as she watched, she could physically see her legs change colour from a healthy pink to a sickly, unnatural grey, and soon after she fell into a coma. During the ordeal, her heart stopped on several occasions.

The doctors told John that there was little they could do for his wife; her vital organs were failing, and they said she had little chance of survival; even if she did make it, they stated, it was likely she would lose both her arms and legs at the very least.

On the advice of others, John had Gill airlifted to a larger hospital in Bangkok that could offer Gill more specialist treatment. It was a chance he had to take – he wasn't willing to give up so easily.

After more tests at the larger, more equipped hospital, Gill was diagnosed with a soil-based gram-negative bacteria, which gave her a rare type of septicemia that was – regardless of the label – never properly identified. The attacking bacteria made all her blood rush into her body to protect her vital organs.

The doctors administered a whole range of antibiotics, and eventually, five weeks later; Gill slowly regained consciousness.

Gill stated that after first watching her legs change colour, and then falling into a coma, she has no recollection of the five weeks.

Although permanently scarred, the doctors managed to save Gill's arms, but had to amputate both her legs below the knees.

John stated the doctor in charged warned him that, "The vast majority of people in her situation, that he came across, in reality, ended up not being able to use their legs and spent the rest of their lives in a wheelchair, because it is extremely difficult to learn to walk again on two prosthetic legs, and it's extremely painful to go through."

Gill left the hospital in a wheelchair on 22nd December 2004, just days before the Indian ocean tsunami hit Phuket.

With the devastating loss of both her legs below the knees, some believed Gill would concentrate on her health and slow down, maybe even give up on helping the animals altogether.

"What some of these animals have been through is horrendous," she states, "and yet they come out the other side totally okay with people again. It's a trait human beings just don't have. Yes, that truly inspires me and keeps me going!"

Gill was fitted with basic prosthetic legs, and she had to learn to walk again.

She received help from one special friend.

Gill has an old blind dog – one of her first rescues – called Ginger, who only has one eye, which she is blind in. As Gill went through extensive physiotherapy, Ginger would be right by her side.

"Whenever Gill went up the stairs on her knees, Ginger would be by her side, step by step, helping her," John said.

Ginger was repaying all the help Gill had shown to her over the years.

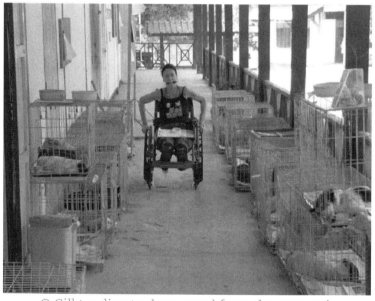

© Gill tending to dogs saved from the tsunami.

A reporter from the BBC *Yorkshire & Lincolnshire*

Inside Out Show, asked Gill in an interview, "Given what happened to you, would you go back into the field to save the dog?"

Without hesitating, Gill responded by saying, "I darted that dog, and if I had chosen not to go in, she would have died – she would have drowned! So if the price I have to pay is to lose my legs, then yes I would do it again!"

Did Gill slow down after she lost both her legs below the knees?

5

THE ASIAN TSUNAMI DEVASTATES PHUKET

Mere days after leaving the hospital in a wheelchair, the Indian ocean tsunami struck.

Phuket, like many other places in the region, was devastated.

The Thai government reported 4,812 confirmed deaths, 8,457 injured, and 4,499 missing after the country was hit by the tsunami. Altogether, Thailand estimates 8,150 are likely to have died in the region. Figures that came out on January 7th 2005 states that in the south region, 5,078 people were reported to have died.

In Phuket, 259 people died, with 105 of those being tourists. With another 1,111 people injured, and 700 reported missing – so the death toll is closer to a thousand.

Sadly, among the casualties was Gill's best friend, Leone Cosens, who cared for hundreds of dogs in the south of Phuket. She died after going to the aid of tourists when the second-wave hit.

For the first three days after the tsunami – even though they had just been through a life-changing ordeal themselves, and no one would blame them if they stayed at home to recover – John and Gill went up to Khao Lak, which had been the hardest hit.

John was involved in sorting and wrapping human remains, while Gill, still in her wheelchair, went to the local hospital to give emotional support to the injured and to relatives of the victims.

Once professional relief teams arrived, John and Gill went back to rescuing and treating the thousands of dogs and cats who had been affected by the tsunami.

Patong Beach, Phuket after the tsunami disaster of December 2004. (Photo from Wikipedia).

The eyes of the world had been focused on

South-East Asia, and this had attracted a number of volunteer vets and nurses who arrived in Phuket to help out at Soi Dog. This meant that at one stage, two or three mobile sterilization clinics were being run simultaneously everyday.

6

THE FIRST SOI DOG SHELTER

As Gill recovered, and eventually learnt to walk again on her prosthetic legs, the three pushed on with the sterilization programme. Gill had no intention of letting her disability get in the way of her work.

A two-year grant from WSPA who had raised a lot of funds because of the tsunami, helped to fund a clinic at a building they rented in Phuket Town, along with two vets and some support staff.

They were still however faced with the problem of what to do with the hundreds of dogs and cats that needed medical treatment and sheltering. Over a hundred such dogs were already at the over-crowded clinic.

The solution came in spring 2006, when Soi Dog was offered the chance to use a government-owned dog pound in the north of the island.

© Gill with friends at the dog pound.

Soi Dog had to spend around three million baht (ninety thousand dollars) to bring the shelter up to standards. There was no treatment clinic, poor drainage, an insufficient outer fence, a lack of runs and kennels, no isolation unit, and no laundry room. All these things had to be addressed.

When the shelter had been brought up to scratch, Soi Dog was able to offer medical treatment to the sick and injured animals, and was also able to shelter them. It was turning into a "full service" operation for the stray animals. In parallel with this, 2006 was the year that Gill started a school's animal welfare education program around the island, to teach children the basics of proper and responsible care for dogs and cats.

© Gill after giving an animal welfare class, Phuket.

Margot returned to Bangkok in 2006, suffering from exhaustion, so it was left to John and Gill to continue the work in Phuket. They were unfortunately given notice by the government to leave the shelter soon after all the improvements had been made, as the government thought it was wrong that an non-government organization should be running a government facility. So in 2008 they moved to a new location in Mai Khao, northern Phuket, where they built runs and kennels, and converted a cattle shed into a clinic, and built store rooms, and a laundry room.

They remain there to this day, housing around four hundred dogs and about forty cats at any one time. They are in the process of building a new dog hospital on the site (2015).

The shelter land is now fully owned by Soi Dog, which currently employs full-time vets, nurses, carers, and animal welfare officers both in Phuket and at its new clinic in Bangkok. The mobile clinic operation also still functions every working day of the week across different parts of Phuket and now adjacent provinces.

© Building work at the new shelter in Mai Khao, Phuket.

In 2008, Gill became the first ever non-Asian to win the coveted Asian of the Year award from Channel News Asia in Singapore, and followed this by being named the Asia Pacific Canine Hero in 2011 at a ceremony in Hong Kong.

As of July 2015, over eighty-eight thousand street dogs and cats had been sterilized since Soi Dog started in 2003 – over seventeen thousand in 2014 alone.

The number of stray dogs on Phuket is now

drastically reduced, with the island being declared Thailand's first officially rabies-free province as a direct result of the sterilization and vaccination programme.

Since 2011, Soi Dog has also been leading the initiative to stop the illegal dog meat trade in Thailand, and in introducing Thailand's first ever animal welfare bill, which became law in December 2014. John was first made aware of the illegal dog meat and skin trade in 2007, and tried to get a number of much larger animal welfare charities to help him address it, but was unsuccessful.

Soi Dog built and finances shelters for dogs destined for the meat and skin industries that have been intercepted by the authorities at a huge complex in Buriram, northern Thailand.

Soi Dog provides all the food and medication for the fifteen hundred dogs housed there as well as other dogs housed at another government facility in the north west of Thailand.

Soi Dog Foundation also financed the renovation of a huge temple shelter called Wat Suan Kaew, on the outskirts of Bangkok, which is home to over a thousand dogs and cats, who were living in sub-standard conditions. Just before Soi Dog's intervenetion, the shelter was described by one international animal welfare organization as, "The worst shelter in the world."

As already stated, by the end of May 2015, the stray population in Phuket was officially under control. This allowed Soi Dog to downscale its operations there, and embark on a similar sterilization and vaccination programme in Bangkok and neighboring provinces of Phuket.

© One of the runs at Buriram (northeastern provinces) home to survivors of the dog meat trade.

A survey carried out by Soi Dog Foundation in May 2015 indicates over six hundred thousand dogs on the streets of Bangkok so it is likely to be a very long programme, but an essential one. Around ten percent of the street dogs in Bangkok carry the rabies virus, according to the Thai Veterinary Medical Association, so it's not just important from a population control perspective.

Both John and Gill remain highly active at Soi Dog to this day.

John leads the foundations fight against Thailand's illegal dog meat trade, and together with its partners in the Asia Canine Protection Alliance (ACPA) it is also addressing the dog meat trade in

Vietnam, Laos, Cambodia, and South Korea.

In 2015, ACPA launched a campaign to end the barbaric dog meat trade in Vietnam, which has been supported by a number of Vietnamese celebrities. The petition has already been signed by over four hundred thousand Vietnamese animal lovers.

Meanwhile, Gill continues as Soi Dog's Global Ambassador, and is currently building a network of local country ambassadors – all famous people in their own right.

Also, Gill has received help from high profile international celebrities such as Ricky Gervais, the music artist/actor Goldie (Clifford Price), the Academy-Award-winning actress Dame Judie Dench, as well as Penelope Wilton, Peter Egan and other Downton Abbey stars, who have donated their time to aid the Soi Dog Foundation. After he visited the shelter in 2015 Gill asked the singer Will Young to be a UK ambassador.

Some of them star in a three minute and forty-seven-second clip, where the celebrities watch the footage of the dogs getting rounded up for transport and more, and then they speak about the atrocities.

Here is the web-address for the YouTube video:

www.youtube.com/watch?v=gerA3kWXEz4

7

THAILAND'S ILLEGAL DOG MEAT TRADE

Not content with all his other responsibilities, John has in addition almost single-handedly been fighting Thailand's illegal trade in dogs, dog meat and dog skin since 2011.

The illegal trade in dogs and dog meat from Thailand to Vietnam, is destined for Hanoi's "fashionable" dog meat restaurants.

Every single stage of this illegal, horrific industry, from sourcing to transit to preparation for death inflicts the most unimaginable pain and suffering on the animals. Dogs are stolen from the streets right throughout Thailand. Many are pets or temple dogs, as these are more trusting than strays, and therefore, easier to catch. They are crammed tightly into small cages, often ten dogs per cage, and loaded onto adapted pick-up trucks, often ten cages per truck. When they arrive at the temporary holding centers in the north of Thailand, many will already have suffocated to death.

© Dogs saved from the illegal dog meat trade in Thailand.

The holding centers, which may host up to two thousand dogs, have an air of death about them. Somehow the dogs seem to sense the fate that awaits them. Here they are graded. The Chinese prefer big dogs, so the large ones are packed tightly into small cages, and shipped north overland. For the small and medium-sized dogs, those in the best condition are earmarked for Vietnam, and the remainder stay in Thailand to be sold to local butchers and tanneries. Those going to Vietnam are stuffed into small metal cages, often ten or more in each cage. The cries and the whimpers are heart-breaking. Limbs and even heads stick through the gaps in the metal bars as the dogs struggle to get breathing space. The cages are slammed next to and on top of each other as the trucks are quickly loaded, resulting in severely injured limbs and terrible head injuries.

© Adapted pick-up trucks for transporting stolen dogs.

Between a hundred and a thousand dogs per truck (depending on vehicle size) would be smuggled across the border via the Mekong River into Laos, before embarking on the long and arduous road trip, sometimes taking up to four days to arrive in Vietnam. During this grueling journey, the dogs would not be fed or watered once.

And it's sad to admit this, but the lucky dogs would be those who died on route as a result of suffocation, thirst, or injuries sustained during loading the trucks. Because the fate that awaits those dogs who did survive the journey can only be described as hell on earth.

Force-fed by pumping rice into their stomachs to increase their weight and value at a village south of Hanoi, a village where the only commercial activity is the dog meat trade and which, in effect, serves as a huge wholesale centre, most of the dogs will eventually end up in Hanoi, at one of the city's many sadistic and grizzly slaughter houses. Some people in Asia mistakenly believe that inflicting pain on dog's releases adrenalin, which tenderizes the meat and improves its flavor. Beating, burning, boiling and skinning dogs alive is not uncommon. Even in countries where eating dogs is not illegal, they are not considered livestock, hence no controls exist to ensure they are killed humanely.

© Dog smuggler's truck at the bank of the Mekong River.

The Thai Veterinary Association estimated in 2011 that around half a million dogs a year were involved in this trade from Thailand to Vietnam, a figure more than confirmed by villagers at the wholesale centre in Vietnam. That would make this illegal industry worth over twenty-five million dollars a year to the organized-crime families that run it.

In 2013, Soi Dog formed the Asia Canine Protection Alliance (ACPA) along with fellow charity's Animals Asia, Change for Animals Foundation and Humane Society International. Following conferences with representatives of the governments of Vietnam, Thailand, Laos and Cambodia in Hanoi and Bangkok, a five-year ban on the importation of live dogs and dog meat was imposed, based on the risk of transmission of rabies. The result of this has been a vast decrease in the number of dogs being trafficked, to such an extent that the trade at one point had almost been wiped out.

However, undaunted the smugglers continue to find other ways to profit from man's best friend. The dog skin industry is thriving, supplying amongst others, manufacturers of golf gloves. New smuggling routes have opened up through the far north of Thailand into Laos and then onto China. It is also believed that the smugglers have established routes from Thailand through Cambodia and then into Vietnam from the south. Dogs are also being killed in Thailand, and their carcasses smuggled into Laos in ice bins for processing, before being forwarded on to Vietnam.

Soi Dog's mission to stop the trade therefore continues. A thousand large posters have been erected throughout north east Thailand, offering rewards for information leading to the arrest of traffickers and butchers, which is proving highly successful. A further thousand will be erected in the far north, and more will go up wherever smuggling routes are being established.

© Soi Dog poster campaign in north east Thailand to stop illegal dog smugglers.

So what happens to the dogs rescued from the illegal dog meat trade? With no government budget to care for them, Soi Dog has built shelters at a centre four hours north of Bangkok, and provides all food and medication for the dogs. It is a costly but necessary exercise, as otherwise the dogs would simply die of starvation or disease, with euthanasia not being an option. Attempts are being made to find homes for these thousands of dogs.

Soi Dog is also working with the Vietnamese border authorities to ensure that no trucks or lorries with live dogs or dog meat are allowed into Vietnam. And in 2015, Soi Dog and its partners that make the

Asia Canine Protection Alliance (ACPA) launched a major campaign in Vietnam to eliminate demand for dog meat. Initiatives are also underway to stop the dog meat trade in South Korea.

There is clearly a lot more work to do before the welfare of dogs and cats in Thailand is raised to an acceptable level. But thanks to people like John and Gill Dalley and the Soi Dog Foundation, huge strides are being made in several key areas.

© Gill demonstrating the cramp cage. This one cage could hold up to ten dogs or more, all forced in.

8

THE TRADE OF SHAME PROGRAMME

For at least the past thirty years a little known trade has existed within Thailand that has seen millions of Thai dogs smuggled illegally to China and Vietnam for human consumption. In addition, hundreds of thousands of dogs are slaughtered within Thailand for their skins and for local consumption. This is an illegal industry, as we have already stated.

Do Thai people agree with eating dogs or with the dog meat trade?

Research has shown that many Thai people do not even know about the trade and ninety percent of people interviewed are totally against it. Dog meat is consumed only in a few areas of Thailand, though there is no way of knowing if dog meat is mixed with other meat and sold to consumers unknowingly, in a similar way that dog meat has been identified in meat offered for sale in Asian restaurants in the west.

What is Buriram?

© A typical run in the Buriram shelters.

Buriram is a province in north east Thailand that is now home to the vast majority of dogs saved from Thailand's illegal dog meat trade. Soi Dog financed the construction of this purpose-built facility follow-ing the successful interception of smugglers trucks loaded with thousands of dogs on their way from Tha Rae in Sakon Nakorn to the banks of the Mekong River, which marks the border with Laos. The shelter is technically a Thai government facility, but Soi Dog paid for its construction, and pays for all the food and medical treatment given to the dogs. The shelter at Buriram homes around one and a half thousand dogs, all saved from the dog meat trade.

How much does it cost to feed and medically treat the dogs at Buriram every month?

It costs Soi Dog around twenty thousand dollars every month to feed and treat the dogs that are saved from the meat trade. That's just over thirteen dollars per dog per month.

9

THAI AND BUDDHIST ATTITUDES TO DOGS AND CATS IN GENERAL

Buddha taught that all sentient beings, including those in the animal realm, possess Buddha nature and therefore can attain enlightenment, and that from infinite rebirths, all animals have been our past relatives; sisters, mothers, brothers, fathers, and children. Therefore, it is against the First Precept to harm, kill or eat sentient beings as it is the same as harming, killing or eating the flesh of our own child or mother. Monks were forbidden from intentionally killing an animal, or drinking water with living creatures (such as larvae) in it.

The Buddhist faith dictates that one must not deliberately kill any living creature either by committing the act oneself, instructing others to kill, or approving of or participating in acts of killing.

The Buddhist faith preaches compassion to all living things. Most Buddhist temples welcome stray dogs to their grounds. The monks feed the dogs with the food donations they get from the local people, and the dogs are generally safe there. The monks know that if the strays were left on the streets to fend for themselves, the lives of the dogs would be significantly worse.

10

WHY ARE THERE SO MANY STREET DOGS?

Think of Thailand and you might conjure up images of golden, stunning Buddhist temples, orange clad monks in procession, white sandy beaches, paddy fields, spicy Thai street food and happy, smiling people. Less commonly associated with the country are severe animal welfare violations, a thriving illegal trade in dogs for meat and skin, and the huge problem of stray and abandoned dogs that blights every beach, village, town and city in the country.

It is impossible to stroll along the picture-perfect beaches without seeing packs of stray dogs fighting for food or dominance. Or thin, sometimes tailless cats hiding down behind restaurant tables looking for dropped food.

Welcome to the land of the street dog.

Conservative estimates suggest that Thailand is home to upwards of ten million street dogs, many of which were born on the streets, and many of which are former companion animals cruelly rejected and abandoned by their owners and left to fend for themselves on the street. Every year, hundreds of thousands more unwanted puppies are born onto the streets. Most will not survive their first month of life. But those who do are sadly destined for a life of hunger, pain, misery and rejection.

It's a very tough life for all of the street dogs, young or old. Food is scarce, and the dogs have to fight almost daily to defend their territories. Sickness and illnesses are rampant because few of the dogs have had vaccinations, and the threat of being poisoned or attacked by humans in their neighborhoods is ever-present. Those dogs whose territories are around hotels or restaurants are the most at risk as owners of these establishments don't want them bothering their guests. Methods used to get rid of the dogs include dowsing in scalding water or oil, poisoning, and attacking with machetes.

The lucky ones are those who find their way to one of the many Buddhist temples in the country. Here they will be fed left-over's from the monk's meals, and will be relatively safe. However, they will receive no medical care, and will remain unsterilized and unvaccinated.

The Thai street dog problem stems from two main issues: Firstly, because of cultural and religious beliefs, most Thais do not sterilize (or vaccinate) their dogs. The Buddhist philosophy is that nature should take its course, meaning that interfering with nature is against most Thai's principles. Unfortunately, this does not just relate to sterilization and vaccination. When companion dogs fall ill, they are frequently left without treatment. The philosophy is known locally as "Buddha's Will." Or in English, "What will be, will be."

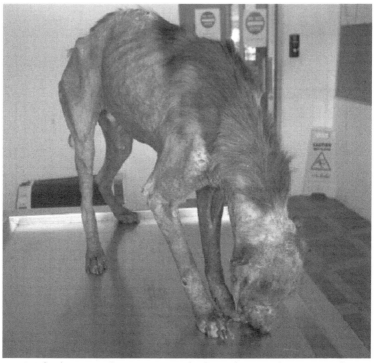

© Thai street dog Hero, a victim of a machete attack.

The second reason for the huge number of street dogs is that whilst the Thai's love puppies, they are less keen on fully grown dogs. Once the puppy becomes an adult, many are simply cast out onto the streets to fend for themselves, and replaced at home by another puppy. Also, black dogs or cats are feared, due to not being able to see the eyes very well, making them seem evil.

Quite apart from the animal welfare issues surrounding street dogs, and the environmental problems caused for humans by the presence of stray dogs, there is also the issue of the spread of disease from stray dogs to human beings. Between fifteen and twenty-five people each year die in excruciating pain from rabies in Thailand, almost exclusively from dog bites. It is estimated that in Bangkok alone, around ten percent of the street dog population carry the rabies virus. Rabies is also a significant problem in several other South East Asian countries, notably Laos, Cambodia and Vietnam.

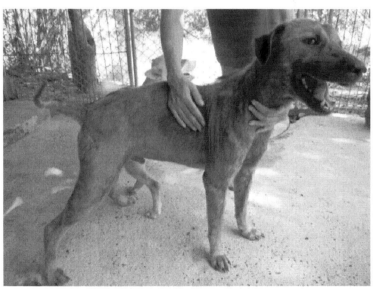
© Hero after treatment at Soi Dog.

So is there an effective solution to the street dog population problem? The only proven sustainable way to control populations of stray dogs is mass sterilization of the animals, coupled with education programmes to teach the general public how to properly care for animals. Sadly, more often than not in countries that have significant stray dog populations, it is left to non-government organizations (NGO) to assume responsibility for addressing the problem. Governments will too frequently complain of a lack of resources.

This was precisely the situation that British couple John and Gill Dalley found themselves in when they retired to Phuket. They were shocked by the sheer numbers and more importantly the plight and welfare of Phuket's street dogs (and cats), and became determined to do something about it, as you have already read.

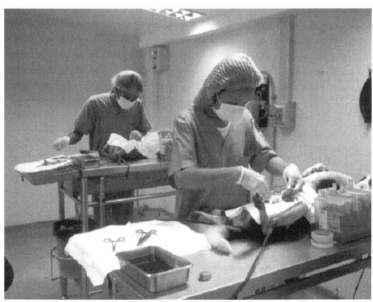

© Sterilization operations at the Soi Dog clinic 2014.

11

NEW SOI DOG PROJECTS FOR 2015

Apart from the mass sterilization and vaccination programme planned for Bangkok, the next priority for Soi Dog is closing down the dog meat trade in Vietnam, which it will do with its partners in the Asia Canine Protection Alliance.

A grassroots campaign is underway with the Vietnamese youth, who are vocally against the trade.

This is supported by a viral video featuring some of Vietnam's most famous pop and movie stars, and two petitions to the government, one Vietnamese and one international, which will target one million signatures each. Clearly, the effort will involve a significant amount of lobbying as well. Similar initiatives will take place in Laos, Cambodia and South Korea in the future, but there will be a slightly different approach for each country.

Also they are in the final stages of building a

new dog hospital at the Phuket shelter. The one and a half million dollar facility is only possible due to the continued support of loyal supporters.

The facilities at the new hospital will include a fully equipped operating theatre, a physiotherapy room, a radiography room, a treatment room, a dental room, a laboratory, a bathing room, 2 examination rooms, a supply room, a food preparation room, an intensive care unit with 8 kennels, an isolation unit with 2 rooms and twenty kennels, a mother and puppy unit with 11 kennels, and 42 main kennels, and a veterinary office.

In chapter 13, I get a tour of the new dog hospital (that is still in progress) by the Project Manager Paul Lloyd.

© The new dog hospital at Soi Dog, Phuket.

A WALKING TOUR OF THE FACILITY

12

A TOUR WITH GLEN JOHNSON

DECIDING TO DO SOME VOLUNTARY WORK

When my brother Gary and I first had the epiphany to give away all our belongings and travel around Asia, we also agreed that we would help out some charitable organizations as we made our way around, a sort of karma boost.

This is possible because I make a living via writing and publishing (my Facebook page is www.facebook.com/GlenJohnsonAuthor). To-date, I have forty-one books published of my own work through Sinuous Mind Books, plus another fifty-one modern-classic fiction books that we publish with our second publishing company called Red Skull Publishing (both are on Facebook). My main bread and butter is The Sixth Extinction Series, which to date is eighteen books long, so the best thing we could offer, to help out, is by helping different charities by writing them a book, to get their story out to as many people as possible, while also leaving them with the royalties, while publishing it for them through Amazon, Barnes & Noble, iTunes, Smashwords, Sony, and dozens of other outlets – in ebook and paperback format.

We contacted charities all over Asia, in Thailand, Malaysia, Sri Lanka, Cambodia, India, and Indonesia, just to name a few, and were surprised at the response.

We short listed the ones we thought would make the best books. They are all worthy charities, but we had to decide, which would make the most interesting stories – stories people would pay to read. We narrowed it down to fourteen organizations.

However, after we arrived in Asia, we let the time slip away, and before we knew it, almost ten months had passed as we traveled from country to country while I continued to pour out my own books.

Then in May 2015, as we returned to Bangkok, Thailand for the third time, as we exited Cambodia after checking out Angkor Wat in Siem Reap, we decided it was time we helped out. We realized there was a charity close by in Phuket that we had been chatting with – a mere eighteen-hour bus ride away.

With a few emails to John and Gill Dalley it was all arranged; we would turn up at Soi Dog Foundation with our backpacks and start the process of creating them a book about all the work they are achieving and what they have planned for the future.

We hopped on a bus from Khaosan Road and headed south.

GETTING TO SOI DOG

We first arrived out of the blue at Soi Dog. Even though we sent a message saying we would be there around 11 am, when traveling around Asia, there is no definite time or location – the system just doesn't work like that over here. Sometimes it can be days either way.

Thailand is a stunning country, but their transport system sucks. It's a kind of organized chaos. We had been over in Asia for almost ten months and had traveled over twelve thousand miles around India, Thailand, Malaysia, Singapore, and Cambodia, by buses, trucks, vans, tuk-tuks, taxis, minibuses, airplanes, and boats, so we knew what to expect and how the system works.

We were shunted from one bus to another, then to smaller minibuses. All we have to identify our final destination is a colorful sticker that was slapped on our chest in Bangkok.

It's complete potluck that you ever arrive on time or in the right destination. However, the system does seem to work.

Phuket is in the south of the country, and is the largest island in Thailand, and has a surface area of just over two hundred and twenty square miles – the second smallest province (Changwat) in Thailand. It also has another thirty-two islands off its coast. At its longest, it is thirty miles long, and thirteen miles at its widest point. Seventy percent of the island is covered in mountains, leaving thirty percent of plains. Sixty percent of the island is covered in forest and rubber and palm oil plantations. It is connected to the mainland by a bridge from the Phang Nga Province. It formerly derived its wealth from tin and rubber, which has now been surpassed by tourism.

Soi Dog is right at the top of Phuket island near the airport, located in the thinnest section.

When I chatted with John via email, he said try to get them to drop you by the airport, it will be cheaper than going all the way down to Phuket Town, and having to catch a taxi back up.

Sage advice.

However, when I asked the minibus driver if he could drop us anywhere near the top of Phuket, just pull over and let us jump out, he gave me a resounding no. It became obvious once we sped past the airport, and down the island. I am fully aware that every mile we head down is now costing me money. The minivan didn't take us to Phuket Town, which we had paid for. It dropped us off at a small travel shop, so they could get a little more money out of us. Apparently, even though we paid to get to Phuket Town, if we wanted to go any further, we had to pay more, (the town was another twenty miles away).

This didn't sit well with the other eight people on our minibus. However, we had been through it all before and knew how the system worked. We had just come from Cambodia, and that is rife with people trying to squeeze just a little more out of you at every single turn, to the point where it starts to get annoying.

So as the Americans, Germans and French people on the minibus shouted and swung their arms around complaining that they had already paid to get to their destinations, we simply collected our backpacks, slung them over our shoulders, and started walking back up the six-lane motorway back towards the airport that was a good ten or so miles away. If anything, we have saved a few miles by being dropped off outside of Phuket Town.

We then took twenty minutes to cross the six lanes of thundering traffic in heat that was touching on forty degrees. Once we got on the right side, we stood waiting for a taxi.

All the way down from the tip of Phuket, there were taxis everywhere – sometimes it seemed like the only vehicles on the roads were taxis. However, sods law, the instant we needed one they all seemed to have vanished.

We waited in the baking sun for almost half an hour before a taxi came into view. I waved my arms as if I had been stranded on a desert island for years and this was a passing, rescue boat.

"How much to get to Soi Dog please?" I asked as sweat streamed down my face soaking my tee-shirt as I leaned into the car through the lowered window. The cold air-conditioned air poured over my hot face.

"Where?"

It turns out that even though it is one of the largest animal shelters in Asia, people who lived right next to it were oblivious to its existence.

I had a scrap of paper that I had written the

address of Soi Dog on, plus the hotel we would be staying at. It was now limp with sweat.

The taxi driver studied my slanted writing that looked like a drunk ant had fallen in an ink pot and then crawled across the paper.

"Eight hundred baht!"

"Seriously?" It had only cost me seven hundred each to make our way down from Bangkok, over five hundred miles away, and he wanted more than that to take us about ten.

I was tired, smelly, hungry, and just wanted to reach my destination. However, I wasn't giving up without a fight.

"Five hundred!"

The small Chinese man stared at me as if waiting for me to raise the price. I didn't.

"Okay!"

The sound of the boot opening was the end of the bartering. We put our heavy backpacks in the boot and climbed into the air-conditioned taxi. The seats were leather and it felt like I was floating on air. It was heaven on earth.

Even though it was only about thirty miles away, it still took three-quarters of an hour to find Soi Dog, and that was after we shot past the sign and had to reverse.

When I saw the orange word's SOI DOG on the black background, my shoulders sagged with relief.

Eighteen hours via two buses, then two minibuses, and a taxi later (with no sleep), we had arrived.

THE SOI DOG FOUNDATION

I was shocked as the taxi rolled up the long gravel drive at how big the facility is. To be honest, I wasn't sure what to expect – there is only so much information you can get through reading a website and dozens of emails, and looking through web page photos.

However, we had been traveling for eighteen hours straight; we were tired, smelly, and a little dehydrated, and all we really wanted to do was shower and get some sleep.

No one seemed to know we were coming.

It turned out Gill's car was in the lot, but no one could find her, and John wasn't on site.

Darren, a burly, longtime volunteer started leading me around, looking for Gill, who was no where to be found. After ten minutes, he phoned John. John was at home, off site, and would jump in his truck and head right over.

We waited by the guest hut with our backpacks and frontpacks as everyone carried on with their normal day around us. The place was a buzz of activity.

Banging, sawing, and the general sound of building work floated over the whole site. We would later find out that a large new dog hospital was being built next to the guest hut. It is a one and a half million dollar facility that would provide much-needed space and equipment.

In the guest hut, everyone was polite, smiling, and happy to introduce themselves. It was now coming up to lunchtime, and the site shuts down for an hour between 12 and 1, so the staff could get a bite to eat and a much-needed break. The guest hut started to fill up with the onsite volunteers.

Dogs barked in the background, with the occasional whine or yelp, trying to get the attention of the people nearby.

Right next to the guest area is the sterilization building, where stray dogs and cats are collected from around Phuket by five Soi Dog trucks, and dropped off, where they are spayed/neutered and dropped back in their original locations.

As we are waiting, and the volunteers filled the hut, we watched the white Soi Dog trucks arrive one after another, the backs filled with nervous dogs, whose little faces quickly peered up through the bars before skittishly vanishing again.

Little did I know at the time, but in a week I would get the chance to go out on a truck with Sanae, a rescue officer and Gill, and watch the whole process from beginning to end, including the operation.

The truck driver opened the large gates to the sterilization section and reversed the truck in, then closed the gates, in case an animal escaped while he was taking it from the truck and placing it in a cage, ready for surgery.

As I was stood up, people kept inviting me into the hut to have a seat. I pointed out that I had been sat in one form or another for eighteen hours, and it was nice to just stand and stretch and try to get my backbone to uncurl.

© The sterilization clinic, with one of the five Soi Dog trucks.

Then a large truck pulled in.

John had arrived.

I had seen John in photos, and numerous YouTube videos about Soi Dog and all the work they have been doing, with the stray dogs and the dog meat trade. It was nice to meet him in person.

We shook hands and introduced ourselves.

John is in his mid-sixties, tall, grey haired, but still fit.

We were then led to a section around the corner, by the runs where the dogs that have been rescued from the dog meat trade are housed as we reintroduced ourselves, and we sat around a concrete bench, with dozens of dogs in a large run behind us, trying to see what we were up to – they were a constant reminder of why we are here.

Gary and I outlined the plan for the book. What it would cover, and how we would distribute it. I said it would be all open at the moment, and as we soaked in the environment, and got to know the facility and people better, the book would evolve depending on how we decided would be the best publication to get as many people's attention as possible, to get the word out about the Soi Dog Foundation.

John is a very down to earth, passionate man. This rung from him like a loud bell as he described what they've achieved so far, and their plans for the future.

John and Gill gave up their retirement and a peaceful existence in Phuket to continue Soi Dog after Margot Homburg returned to Bangkok, and kept it running after it had grown into the largest animal welfare foundation in Asia, and even though I was bone tired, his zeal was contagious.

We were introduced to Martin, the man responsible for everything that goes out to the media (he is the foundations Media Officer). He asked for my email and said he would send me some press release information about Soi Dog.

In the distance, volunteers walked past with dogs walking calmly on the end of leads. Vets and clinic aids walked past in blue scrubs. We also caught a glimpse of Gill with hands full of paperwork, busy with the new dog hospital. Burmese staff, in their orange Soi Dog shirts were everywhere, all happy and smiling. It seemed that everyone who was on site was happy to be here.

After chatting for over half an hour John could

see we were waning from lack of sleep. He told us to put our stuff in his truck, and he would personally drop us off at the hotel.

By the time we got to the hotel, and I sorted myself out and eventually logged online, the pile of information from Martin was already sitting in my Inbox.

THE HOTEL

There is a special arrangement with Pensiri House, which classes itself as a budget guesthouse style hotel. However, in reality, it is a stunning hotel – the best we have stayed at in our ten-month trip so far. The hotel has large, air-conditioned rooms (our room is thirty-one square meters), with en-suite, a patio, fridge, safe, a table and chair (good for writing) and is cleaned daily by helpful, cheerful staff, who are always on hand. There are also a small café and shop on site, and they own a phenomenal restaurant right down on Nai Yang beach, and if you show them your room key, you will get ten percent off your meal – bargain.

Soi Dog has an arrangement with Pensiri House, and most volunteers stay here, mainly because in the morning at 8:45 am a truck arrives outside the front door to pick up all the volunteers for free to deliver them to the Soi Dog Foundation complex.

We were completely rejuvenated by a great nights sleep and ready for our first day at Soi Dog. To be honest, the hotel room was so nice I could have kicked back and relaxed on the patio for a week.

However, we had made a commitment, and after seeing Soi Dog, we just wanted to get there to start the book.

© Pensiri House – our double room (home is where you lay your hat).

IN THE TRUCK ON THE WAY TO SOI DOG

We have a kind of nervous excitement when we rise at 8 am to get ready.

Apart from having to get up early if we have to catch a bus or plane, we never have to do early mornings. I am a night owl, and stay up writing to around 3 or 4 am each night (or morning), so I'm not too good with 8 am.

Pensiri Hotel has two main sections – the reception area, with the café and shop, with rooms above, and across a patch of land (car park) is the three-story building where we were staying.

We amble across, nervous about meeting new people. I am an introvert. I don't mind talking and interacting with people, but it has to be on my terms – Gary is even worse.

There are about ten people, males and females (mostly females) waiting for the truck to pick us up. There was shy, hellos, mainly because everyone was so tired.

Two trucks arrived, a pickup and a truck with a cage over the back. The older volunteers got into the air-conditioned cab, while the younger ones jumped in the back of the truck, onto two seats that run down both sides. The driver is a very friendly Thai man called Pond Akkarin, who speaks good English and always has a smile on his face.

As we bounced along, jolting and swinging from side to side, I realized this must be what the animals felt like when they were put in the truck. A horrible feeling overcame me, realizing most animals that enter the trucks are neutered!

We traveled past countless building sites, (it seems the area is up-and-coming) hotels and guesthouses and people's homes, and then the vast airport, with its mile-long grey, galvanized fence that looks like it belongs to a prison compound, that runs the length of the single runway. The island is so green, with lush palm trees everywhere. Water buffalos are dotted in every field, heads down chewing the flora. There are also lots of stray animals everywhere, reminding me of why we are here.

Even though it is early, warm air blew in, tossing hair and flapping clothes. I was already soaked in sweat. It dawned on me that I would be spending a whole day without air-conditioning.

I started chatting to the other volunteers.

There is a lady from Melbourne, Australia called Maurita Rahn, who is a slight woman with bright-eyes and blonde hair. It is hard to guess her age. I would say between thirty and forty (best not ask a woman her age when you first meet). It turns out; she had arrived directly from another part of Thailand, where she had been helping out in the Wildlife Refuge, working alongside rescued elephants. She was now spending a few weeks at Soi Dog.

There is also Jess Henderson, a twenty-four-year-old hairdresser from Falkland, Fife, Scotland. Anna Sofie, a twenty-four-year-old from Celle, Germany who has been volunteering as a tour guide for two months. Lou Southgate, also a twenty-four years-old female who works in an animal rescue center called *Poppies Place Animal Rescue* from Essex, England. And lastly (in the back of the truck) Jessie Crawley, also a twenty-one-year-old female volunteer from Aberdeenshire, Scotland, (Jessie's story is covered in chapter 29).

The truck stopped once to pick up one more person, a forty-seven-year-old man called Thomas Schmidt, a German, who had been volunteering for the past few weeks, who was staying at a different hotel. I noticed he had a tattoo on each forearm. On one arm, it read: I love dogs, on the other is read: I love cats – each had a paw print next to them.

We left the main motorway and headed down a thin side road. The sign for Soi Dog was attached to a post, stating it was a 500 meters down the lane.

I had been here the day before in the taxi. However, I was tired and most of the information going in faded due to exhaustion. Also, the truck was much different – a bone jarring ride compared to the air-conditioned taxi.

Soon we arrived at the long black wall with the bright orange Soi Dog logo.

We had arrived.

THE SOI DOG FOUNDATION

We all got out and headed into the guest hut.

The guest hut has a roof to keep out the rain and sun, with two long tables, crowded with plastic chairs. It has a large flat screen TV for showing videos to the volunteers and visitors. Also a donations box, a hot-water dispenser for tea or coffee, a volunteer notice board, a water cooler, and a row of merchandise hanging from hooks, all with the Soi Dog logo, and a single standing fan.

One table is stacked with five white folders – (two) Volunteers Stories, Volunteer's photos, Volunteers Guide, and Shelter inventory, which is full of all the animals on site, along with their information. The names are colour coded, depicting if they have been adopted, etc.

This area is looked after by a longtime volunteer called Diana – a very polite, smiling, happy lady who makes you feel very welcome.

The hut is attached to the kitchen. It contains the hotplate, fridge (filled with cold drinks and chocolate bars – that you can purchase), a sink, a bookshelf, and other miscellaneous items.

The regular volunteers caught up with their night's activity, while collecting their volunteer bags off hooks on the wall. They made coffee, or tea, or fill their bottles from a cold-water dispenser and then sat for a few minutes to get ready for the day ahead.

Gary and I nervously hang in the background.

We were passed a clipboard and asked if we wanted any lunch? There is a menu, and you simply picked what you wanted, dropped the cash into a tub, and it would be delivered at lunchtime. I went for sweet and sour pork, and Gary picked chicken and vegetables.

A thin, thirty-one-year-old German lady called Inga Annika introduced herself and said she was one of the tour guides. Also, if we were volunteering, we had to be taken on a tour, then watch some videos and then sign a form. We would then be assigned a Run or position that fit our abilities.

I stated we weren't run-of-the-mill volunteers that we were here to write a book. The information had yet to dribble down from upon high.

After being there for the day I understood the misunderstanding – the animals are everything, the whole reason everyone is here. A writer from England is not the top priority.

She wasn't sure what to do with us.

We stated we were there to look around for the day, and to take notes and get the general feel for the whole foundation and day-to-day running of the facility.

We were still deciding on what style to write the

book.

Inga stated the first tour was at 9:30, so we had half an hour to wait.

I got out my notepad and started to scribble down our morning so far. The heat is unbearable, so bringing my laptop along to tap away at was out of the question – it would overheat in half an hour. It is strange using a pen and paper, something I haven't done in a while. It made my fingers ache.

Within minutes, a Soi Dog truck arrived to drop off the first stray dogs of the day. The white van reversed into the sterilization building.

Opposite the hut I sat in is the Burmese housing block. A series of rooms on two levels housed the paid staff. I was told they were like a large, happy family. They are all Burmese because, apparently, the Thai people don't like working with stray animals.

The Burmese staff – in bright orange shirts – were everywhere. They all look happy and content, and they were all busy. They also wear a kind of pink clay on their faces – no one I asked knew why? Traditional decoration, or practical for keeping off the sun?

Inga stepped up to announce it was time for our special tour. We would get to see areas the average volunteer didn't.

Inga is German, with a slight accent, and looks like a gymnast, and always wears large sunglasses, and black clothes with the orange Soi logo on the tee-shirt. She looks like she's about to run a marathon.

Inga states, after my questioning that she has

been volunteering since last November.

The tour starts from the hut, and we head right, around the car park, where a line of white Soi Dog cars are parked, along with a few Soi Dog white trucks.

She states that the sterilization of the dogs on the island has been so successful that the five trucks are back at the main foundation complex for the next few weeks until they are moved to new locations around Thailand.

We stop in front of a long linked fence.

To the left is the A Runs, to the right is the B Runs. Both sections have four Runs, each with up to twenty dogs. In the middle is the Enrichment Area, where a dog can be taken and released off the lead, to socialize with the volunteer.

A young female volunteer exited the gate that led to the A and B Runs with a very chubby brown Labrador mutt. The dog is literally wobbling from side to side. My first thought is, *well, that doesn't look neglected. It looks overweight*, as if it's been too well cared for.

Inga must have read my mind.

"She looks fat, because she was force fed by the illegal dog meat trade. They would get more money for her like this. Rice would be forcefully poured down her throat, and she was kept in a cage where she couldn't move to burn off the food."

We are told the (up to) twenty dogs in each Run are in a pecking order, and each Run has an alpha male and alpha female. If we were assigned to a Run, we would soon learn who the boss is, and that would be the first dog to be taken for a walk.

We were told that over one and a half thousand dogs were being held in a large compound up country in Buriram built by Soi Dog, which had all been saved from the illegal dog meat trade. It was supported by Soi Dogs at the cost of twenty thousand dollars a month – around thirteen dollars for each dog.

© The B Runs. A photo taken from the top of the water tower. My legs were shaking while taking this.

We continued around the site.

To one side are large metal containers; the sort you see on the back of trucks, or stacked on a cargo ship. Inga states that thousands of old towels and sheets are donated by hotels, and they are stored in the containers. They are used for bedding and cleaning.

We walk past a shed that has an open side. A

Burmese man is knelt on the ground working on an engine of some sort. He gives us a thousand watt smile.

We come upon a huge manmade lake. The water is an amazing colour. I looked online at Dulux swatches, and I found it described as *Turquoise Treasure*. It has a white duck house floating on it.

© The dog walking area, around the lake.

This, we are told, is the dog walking area. The volunteers walk the dogs clockwise around the lake.

A few people are slowly walking dogs around. They are evenly spaced, due to the animals being from different runs, and not wanting them to become stressed or fight.

We head past the shelter manager's office, which has its own garden with about five or six dogs in. These are the manager's own pets. They are rowdy and loud, and bound over to watch us walk by.

We arrive at a section where most people walk around to the Puppy Run. However, due to getting a

VIP tour, we are walked through the Dog Meat Trade Run (where all the dogs have been rescued from trucks heading over the border) down past the animal's kennels, and into the Skin Problem Run, where the dogs all suffer from various skin conditions and have been separated from the other animals.

The main problem is mange. Mange is a parasitic mite that imbeds itself in either the skin or the hair follicles. It can be treated, but sometimes leaves the animal with just tufts of hair that sometimes grows back, other times it doesn't.

There is one dog that instantly catches my attention. He is called Chinnamon. His name was supposed to be Cinnamon, but due to a spelling error, that stuck, he ended up with a H he shouldn't have.

© Chinnamon, from the Skin Problem Run.

Even though Chinnamon has been cured, his hair has never grown back. However, he seems happy and content, and doesn't seem to notice he is *naked*. Even though the dogs have been cured, they are kept together in one run because other dogs seem to take a disliking to them, and they get picked on.

I heard, just after I left to head to Malaysia that Chinnamon has been adopted by a family in New York, and after just two months, and a change of environment, his hair has completely grown back.

© Inga with some of the OAPs.

We then head into the OAP Run A (there are two OAP Runs), where the older dogs are kept. They slowly amble over on arthritic knees. The older dogs are kept in their own run, so they don't have to put up with the antics of the more boisterous younger animals.

Next it's into the hectic Puppy Run.

The instant the second gate is open (there are two gates to every run, so there is a catchment area in case a dog races past you as you enter. There is also a sanitary hand wash dispenser at every gate) we are inundated with clambering paws and nipping jaws. The small puppies' dive and jump and spring around as if they have jet packs in their backsides, all yapping and barking and clambering for attention. One animal, a German Alsatian cross instantly takes a liking to me, and won't leave me a lone. Another puppy starts to try to chew my bracelets off my arm.

© A little puppy chewing on my bracelets.

A couple stay around our feet, begging for attention, while the rest scatter to every corner of the run, jumping, rolling and climbing. One beige puppy sits perfectly still in a huge plastic water tub, with the water up to his shoulders. He looks very happy cooling down in the water. The temperature is 36 °C (just under 100 °F). I'm hot and sweating profusely; I can't imagine how hot he is, with his little fur coat on?

Inga stands while cradling a puppy in her arms, with its feet in the air as she strokes his belly.

We exit the Puppy Run and continue.

All the puppies gather at the gate, whining, and giving us sad eyes for leaving them. I wish I could keep them all. But within seconds, they have forgotten all about us and continue racing around their run.

On the right is the Shy Dog Run, where all the shy, unsure dogs are kept. Ones that are picked on for being too quiet by the other dogs.

Next to that is the Small Dog Run, where the smaller animals are kept. It's unfair to put them in runs with the dog two or three times their size. They seem content being with other dogs their own size. There aren't that many small dogs because Thai people seem to prefer their pets smaller.

Then we pass the office. At least a dozen people sit at computers. The sound of clacking keyboards rings out of the open windows. This is the backbone of Soi Dog, where the volunteers keep the website and Facebook pages up-to-date, and arrange adoption papers, and everything else that is needed that has made Soi Dog the largest animal welfare shelter in Asia.

We pass the Hotel Run, where dogs that have

been adopted are awaiting their flights to new homes. They have to wait three months after their last blood test before they can be put on an outboard flight.

On the right is the new dog hospital that is being finished off. Thai builders swarm the structure, hammering, or laying bricks, or tiles. I am told it should be ready for December, and that it cost just over one and half-million dollars for the building, and all the equipment it will house, making it the most up-to-date, technologically advanced clinic in southeast Asia.

My first thought is, *They must be doing something right. One and a half million dollars is not a number to be sniffed at, and all from voluntary contributions and fundraising.*

Then we enter the cat complex.

© The cat treatment area. Once they have been passed, they move to another room. Mui checking on some kittens.

The cats have their own air-conditioned

building. There are two main runs, along with the clinics for treating the cats. The runs have inside and outside sections.

Later, I had time to come back and sit with the cats in Run B for an hour. Within minutes, I have a cat blanket, with five of them on me.

The room is the coldest place on site, with air-conditioning and fans. Cats are strewn everywhere, as if giant hands picked up a bunch of them and gently scattered them around the room. Some on the floor, against the walls, on shelves, in baskets attached high on a wall, and some standing, and meowing, by the sliding glass door waiting for someone to come and stroke them.

Sadly, a few have only three legs, due to animal cruelty. The three-legged cats are a little shy – understandably. I had two three-legged cats come over to check me out. One was black and called Savoy, who cuddled behind my back, between me and the wall, and another (after half an hour, when it realized it could trust me) tried to get on my shoulder – which was hard, because it couldn't climb very well. A lot of clawing was involved. When it reached the summit of my shoulder, it settled down, content to watch everything from its new advantage point and commenced purring as loud as a jet engine into my right ear.

There is one large adult black cat that is covered in scars and patches of no fur, called Jerker. He is very cautious and inches closer over a three quarter of an hour period, while checking my every move-ment. Eventually, he rested lying against my leg and allows me to rub his chin.

They all have flea collars on, with their names on them.

There's Mittens, a grey mottled kitten that moves very slowly and cautiously that has the largest eyes I've ever seen on a cat before, and can outstare a statue. A completely opposite character is Rolex, a white Siamese looking kitten that is hyperactive and never stops moving over me, and head-butting me for attention, and she likes to chew on fingers.

Outside the large sliding glass door is a long corridor, where Cat Run A is located as well as rooms for treating the cats, and some for housing the poorly while they recuperate.

As I sit on the tiled floor, while cats used me as a climbing frame, I watched a young couple who were stood inside an operating room, who had just brought in a stray cat they had found. The cat was quickly put on the metal table, and the vet started sorting out whatever the problem was.

A Burmese lady, in an orange Soi Dog shirt, was running back and forth with equipment, as she helped the vet. Within ten minutes, the couple had left and the cat was removed and placed in the Recovery Room.

Another animal was helped while I sat and watched from across the corridor.

The speed and efficiency that the vet and assistant worked was amazing to watch. They are so confident. There were no awkward movements or standing around, it was utter professionalism.

Back to the tour.

Inga walked me back to the Guest Hut and

prepared the TV for some videos for us to watch.

Gary was still with me, but he stands in the background quietly, soaking it all in like a sponge while taking photos.

The first video is for all volunteers to watch and goes over the basics – how to deal with the dogs in the runs, walking them, where to walk them, how to act if some start to fight while you're in the run with them, if they get off the lead or out of the run, and what is inside your volunteer bag, etc.

Most is common sense.

The volunteers each receives a waterproof bag which belongs to the run they have been assigned to. Each bag contains a dog brush, three leads, (not to walk three at once, but in case some dogs escape the run when you open the gate. So you tie the one you're walking to the side, then one at a time you put a lead on an escapee and take it back to the run), and a folder containing all the information about each dog in their run.

We then watch some more videos.

One was about rehoming the animals with Alex in. Alex used to be a flight attendant, before volunteering at Soi Dog. She is now a permanent resident, and has the perfect, authoritative, English accent for the instruction videos. (Alex's Story is covered in chapter 23).

One video was with John Dalley narrating; all about the dog meat trade that he has been lobbying and fighting against for years – which has made a huge difference, saving thousands of animals from a horrendous, painful death. We watched as cages full of whining dogs are stacked on the back of a truck. It is heartbreaking to witness.

With a tear in my eye, I realized it was lunchtime, as the other volunteers started to return to the guest hut.

LUNCHTIME AND SOME VISITORS

The hut soon filled up with faces I recognized. They started handing out lunch. I was impressed with my sweet and sour pork – the meat was tender and there was plenty of it. I purchased a coke from the kitchen area. It is an honor-system. If you take something from the fridge, you leave the correct money in a plastic tub.

At about 12:30 an American, middle-aged, woman arrived. She had seen Soi Dog on Tripadvisor and wanted to check it out to see why it is classed as the number-one attraction on the island. Sadly, she arrived at lunchtime, and due to no one being allowed in the runs between 12 and 1; she sat with all the volunteers and chatted with them all. She was made to feel very welcome.

Even though it was lunchtime the rescue trucks continued to arrive one after another and drop-off animals at the sterilization clinic.

When lunchtime was over, Inga took the American lady on a tour. The volunteers broke up to head back to walking the dogs, and I sat catching up on my notes, trying to remember everything Inga told me on the way around.

Another person arrived. Her name is Kate Petersen, and she is a thirty-three-year-old, a tall thin, woman from Maine, USA with a pale complexion and light hair, and bright intelligent eyes. She is halfway through her veterinarian degree, and she had arrived to help out for two weeks while she is in Thailand on holiday. Kate states when she finishes her degree, she wants to go into shelter welfare.

Kate sat and chatted with Inga, after she returned with the American visitor, who had just purchased some Soi Dog merchandise.

Kate chatted with Inga, telling her story, and she was then shown some of the videos.

Within minutes of Kate sitting down to watch the instruction videos, another person arrived. A young woman, originally from South Carolina, USA, (I missed her name) said she lives in Phuket and is in-between jobs and has two months spare where she can help out around the complex.

To one side, an animal welfare officer is hosing out the back of his truck.

Inga chats with the new woman.

Inside the sterilization unit, three Burmese men are moving dogs from one cage to another.

A scooter arrives with a man driving, with a large woman on the back clutching a container holding a dog. I thought she was here to seek help for her animal. It turns out the motorbike is a taxi, and he arrived here thinking Soi Dog was the airport. Donna explains their mistake, and they set off again.

As they pull out two trucks are driving in. One is a Soi Animal welfare officer, with numerous loose dogs in the back, nervously looking up over the sides, before quickly vanishing again. The other truck is a man who has arrived with a stray dog he found that is wounded. The dog is quickly rushed straight into the clinic for emergency treatment.

Through the chain-link gate of the sterilization unit, I watch a young Burmese lady wander around with a clipboard, taking notes about the cats and dogs in the cages.

I'm surprised at all the activity; it's nonstop.

An American couple arrive with their child. They dropped their dog off to be sterilized. The dog was so happy to see its owners. The couple left a contribution in the donation's box.

Gill arrived with a host of people and took over one of the long tables. It was the building committee, arriving to go over details of the new dog hospital build.

I heard Gill ask things like, "Yes, but is that per foot, or meter?" And, in an exasperated tone, "Why put that price down if we can't get it for that price?" It sounded like working with Thai builders was an uphill struggle.

John arrived to join in.

In the distance, a Burmese young man in an orange Soi Dog shirt was taking an old three-legged dog for a very slow walk. Ten minutes later, he walked back the way he had come, carrying the animal – obviously the dog had decided *I have walked far enough, and if you want me to go any further, you'll have to carry me.*

I spent the remainder of the day wandering taking photos, and going back to sit in the Cat Runs, A and B. Then I went to the Small Dogs Run, and then the Puppy Run.

I couldn't believe how fast the day had gone. I was at Soi Dog for eight hours. The time had flown past.

Before I knew what time it was, Pond arrived to ferry us all back to our hotels.

I was excited, because in a few days I would be going out with an animal welfare officer and experiencing catching a stray dog, and bringing it back to have it neutered in the Sterilization Clinic.

However, I would also be given a VIP tour around the new dog hospital that is under construction.

13

A TOUR OF THE NEW DOG HOSPITAL

Today I'm getting a personal tour around the new one and a half million dollar dog hospital, which is in its final stages of construction. The whole project has been possible due to continued support and donations from loyal supporters of the foundation.

I'm excited.

The building is large and obviously people can't just wander around without permission and a guide, due to building regulations and safety.

Ever since I arrived, I have wondered what the inside looks like. Now I am about to find out.

My liaison at Soi Dog is a man called Martin Turner, who is the Media Officer for the foundation. Everything that goes out to the public first has to pass inspection via Martin.

Martin is a forty-six-year-old man who has been working at Soi Dog for just over a year. He is friendly, polite, and is very good at his job. He makes me feel very welcome and puts me at ease. I already feel like I know Martin due to all the emails we have exchanged. (Martin's full story is covered in chapter 27).

Martin arranged for the building project manager, Paul Lloyd to take me on a guided tour of the new dog hospital.

Paul has been instrumental in the new build at Soi Dog. He is accompanied by his long term partner Jan Evans. (You can read more about Paul and Jan's Story in chapter 28).

I wait in the guest hut for Paul.

It is pouring down with rain. That's what I get for visiting during the rainy season.

Thailand's weather is classed as hot and humid with a long monsoon season. It falls into three categories – hot, cool, and wet. The hot season runs from March to June, with April and May being the hottest months.

Depending on what part of the country you are in, the wet season can vary, and the season can fluctuate from year to year, starting sooner or later. However, once it arrives, there is heavy rain accompanied by rough seas.

On the Anderman Sea near Phuket, the wet season can start as early as April or May even though it officially doesn't start until June and runs as late as October. Sometimes in Phuket, the rain doesn't end until late November.

It is raining now; the rain is hammering on the hut's roof.

Around me, on the tables, volunteers sit folding

gauze for the vets. A large pile sits in the center of the table as they fold them one at a time. Even though it is raining, and cooler than normal, and the ground outside is covered in deep puddles, they are happy to be helping. Sadly, it is too wet to walk the dogs.

I have seen Paul numerous times, walking around with Gill and working on the tables with the building committee, but I am yet to meet him personally.

Paul takes long strides across the wet ground, with his head down. He is wearing a large style Australian hat.

He arrives with Martin, who officially introduces us. We briskly shake hands. It is apparent he is a builder; he has a strong vise-like grip.

I was halfway through making a coffee, so Paul joins me.

The rain echoes off the roof. The volunteers laugh and talk amongst themselves, chatting about the dogs in the different runs. The sound of building work rings across the facility. Dogs bark in the background. The sound of Burmese drifts from a group of Burmese staff that are walking past in their bright orange tops.

We swap pleasantries. I like meeting new people, but I am always a little awkward and never know quite what to say. I normally write fiction, and everything comes out of my imagination; I'm not used to doing interviews with real people – I normally let them do most of the talking, and I watch them like a hawk and listen to every word.

As we stand, looking across the grounds, sipping

steaming coffee, I ask how different it is working with Thai builders? I thought I would break the ice with some casual questions.

Paul smiles.

"The worst part is the difference in standards that I am used to," Paul states. "Having worked under British regulations for decades, having to adjust to Thai building standards has been a learning curve."

For example, he explains that the new dog hospital building is supported by one hundred and eight main columns, of various sizes. Once they were completed and checked, a large percentage were condemned. Some were the wrong thickness, others the wrong mix of C40 concrete, and some were even in the wrong location. Once they were replaced and rechecked, some were once again condemned.

He states that the Thai builders need constant supervision to check that the work is up to international standards and is the quality Soi Dog expects – and is paying for – and also to stop unwanted problems in the future.

Another example is, the Soi Dog building committee were not happy with their original electric plans that lacked detail, and they were not sure if the wiring would be up to international standard, so the committee hired an independent electric company consultant to redraw the electrical plans, and carry out regular inspections to ensure the work would be up to standard. Soi Dog offered the contractors building the dog hospital the oppor- tunity to strike electrics out of their costs and that if they were not able to do the work to this standard, then Soi Dog would bring in other electricians.

No need, they were told, we have fully qualified electricians on our staff that can do the job required.

To make things interesting, two years ago the colours for Thai electrical wiring changed. The wiring colours are now earth green, neutral blue, phase one brown, phase two black, and phase three grey.

Paul states the new dog hospital consists of a three-phase electrical setup, and the backup generator power.

This complicates things.

Once some of the wiring was finished an independent inspector arrived to check the quality of the work. The inspector found every wire he checked that should have been brown or grey was white.

Once they got the Thai electrician in front of them to question, it turned out the day he went to buy the brown and grey coloured wires, they only had white in stock. So he did them all in white.

"This is the kind of thing we are constantly up against," Paul explains as he sips his coffee.

We finished our drinks, and Paul asks me to follow him. We exit the dry hut and head through the deep puddles.

I stupidly wore flip-flops today. Even though it is wet, it is still humid and hot. Once my flip-flops get wet my feet slide around like wet fish. It suddenly occurs to me that I will be walking through an active building site with no feet protection.

The new building is right next to the guest hut, so it is a short trip.

The dog hospital is huge and raised up on thick

columns. Around the base is what has been dubbed the *moat* by Ray, who takes the photos – it is a waterway that surrounds the building. There is a wide overhanging lip all the way around the building with no gutters – the water, at present, runs straight off into the *moat*, which is useful during the heavy rain.

It is pouring down now, and water gushes over the side of the building, frothing the *moat* below.

However, this is only temporary, and the crude *moat* around the building, once completed, will be a deep concrete gully, topped with metal grating and landscaped to match the surrounding lawns, and the runoff water from the roof, and surrounding area, will end up in the large artificial lake.

At present, the system is half completed and not yet connected with the lake, so in heavy rain it fills quickly covering the part constructed gulleys. So when anyone needs to cross they lay down boards. The boards are raised and lowered like a drawbridge, hence why the unfinished watercourse is called the *moat*, and the hospital the *castle*.

I walk over a few wooden boards (the *drawbridge*) that cross the *moat*, then up to some concrete steps to the main entrance. To the right is a long ramp, which will enable easy access for trolleys.

There are tools, empty bags, concrete blocks, broken tiles, and sloppy wet mud and concrete rubble piled high as we walk past up to the steps.

Everything is bare concrete. There are large gaps where the windows and doors will be. Large piles of tiles and sacks full of concrete mix are stacked against the bare walls.

"All this front wall will be black tiles with the orange Soi Dog logo," Paul states as he sweeps a hand across the surface.

"Altogether, there will be 2,800 square meters of wall tiles, and 600 square meters of floor tiles in the structure."

That's a lot of tiles; I think to myself.

"That's one of my other main jobs, to check the tilers are leaving a 2 mm gap for the grouting."

We enter through a wide entrance.

Everything is barebones – concrete walls and floors, with wires hanging from uncapped sockets and from above. Air-conditioning ducts rest on metal struts, and five main wire conduit's race along above.

Paul explains about a charity in England that has been kind enough to help them.

"They are called The UK Dogs Trust, and they have twenty sites all around the UK. Gill dealt with their very helpful architect, Matthew Taylor via email and Skype, about how they operated their kennels with regards to the guillotine doors and specialist drain runs. And when I was back in the UK last summer, I arranged to visit some of their centers. They were extremely hospitable and showed me around, and I took photos of their drains and guillotine doors in action at their Shrewsbury Center, which I then sent back to Gill. I also went to the Technik factory near Telford to meet a man called Matthew Rees, who helped us enormously with our requirements and design. I have also called them four times since returning to Thailand, to make sure we are getting exactly what we need."

Sparks dropped down from above. I could see some tanned flip-flopped feet dangling from a wall.

No sturdy, steel toe-capped work boots here.

A face looks over the side. Instead of a welding mask, he has a cloth wrapped around his face, and he is wearing sunglasses.

I have to remind myself that I'm not in England – laws and standards are different here.

Paul said one incident jumps to mind when a group of workers sat astride the main beams, welding. In the distance, thunder rumbled and jagged lightening appeared. It was a powerful storm that was getting closer by the minute. A volley of lightening bolts started furrowing the fields in Mai Khao, adjacent to the site, blasting up soil and debris. Paul said he could feel the thunder vibrating through his chest it was so loud and close.

The workers seemed completely oblivious to the gathering storm that was bearing down on them, and continued working, sat perched on a thick metal beam.

Paul started to run around, waving his arms, and shouting for the workers to get off the roof, away from anything metal. He got no response. However, the workers started to climb down from the roof when torrential rain washed over the building site. A mere sixty seconds after the last reached safety, an earthshaking rumble accompanied by a blinding flash announced a lightening bolt had just struck the apex of the building. Luckily, no one was hurt.

Music drifts through the building, along with the sound of the workers. The clanging of metal on metal, and the whirring and buzzing of saws and drill's rings around us.

Paul sweeps a hand from one side to another as we walk through the building. Empty shells of rooms are all around us.

"Everything in the building has to be metal or concrete. There is no wood anywhere, due to humidity and termites."

Skinny shirtless Thai and Burmese workers are everywhere – tiling, shoveling, drilling, and carrying buckets of concrete or boxes of tiles. They all smile a thousand watt smile with perfect teeth. They all nod and give a greeting. They scramble everywhere like worker ants. A couple of men are sat on the floor cutting tiles. One man is up a ladder. Another is up near the roof.

They probably wonder who I am, following the Project Manager around with a note pad in my hand, scribbling notes.

A random older lady walks past down the corridor, with an umbrella in hand, and she is dressed as if she was walking down a main street. She nods, says, "Sawasdee kha" (a greeting) and vanishes around a corner. Paul doesn't see it as unusual, so I don't ask.

As we walk from room to room, Paul describes what the room will be, and where there will be computer monitors, wall screens, x-ray equipment, pull down tables, Internet connections, plugs, large sinks, store rooms, etc.

I had no idea it was so big inside; it's like Dr. Who's Tardis.

The construction and the idea behind it all is impressive. Soon it will help thousands of animals each month – all from Gill and John's dream to help the street dogs and cats of Thailand.

There's a reception area with a large floor-mounted weighing machine, (another one is outside the x-ray room). A room to one side for the vets which will have six wall mounted monitors, so they can access all the required information they need.

Isolation units, which will have an up-to-date negative and positive air flow system, to keep any infectious diseases away from the rest of the animals, as well as UV lighting that will come on at different intervals at night to help kill airborne bacteria – but only in the x-ray, operation, dental, examination, and treatment rooms, not in any sections where there will be live animals, they don't want to cook them.

A thick-walled x-ray room, which will save them having to send animals to local vets, saving time and money.

There will be a state-of-the-art operating theater for Dr. Katherine, for cases like amputations or bone restructuring. The room will also be sterilized with UV lighting, and there will be a large medical hanging light unit imported from the UK that cost over £3,000, as well as a large monitor on one wall to help with x-ray images and information about whatever animal is on the operating table. A double-walled, sliding unit will be used to pass through equipment that has been sterilized by medical staff in the autoclaves prep area, to the doctor while she works.

There will be a fully equipped drugs room with everything registered on the computers against one wall, with a sliding ladder to access the higher shelves.

A dental room to keep the animals orally healthy.

In one room will be physiotherapy and hydro-therapy. Water therapy is used to help animals that have had orthopedic surgery, lost limbs, and other movement problems. The machine is a pool which can have the water raised or lowered depending on the animal's size, and has a treadmill below the water to rehabilitate the dog.

"Normally," Paul states, "Technik sends their own fitters to install and commission the hydro therapy unit, but we worked out the cost of the flights and accommodation, and it was just too high. So instead, while I was in England, I went to the factory for two days and worked with their fitters to learn how to do it myself." He rubbed his head under the hat. "However, that was over a year ago now, so I just hope I can read my notes and remember everything they told me when it comes to install it."

Luckily, Rachel Bean RVN, a qualified veterinary nurse of eighteen years, will be flying to Soi Dog to volunteer – she will teach the veterinary staff how to use the equipment.

In the treatment room there will be three fold down tables and a fixed wet table for the dogs daily treatment. Also, a large oxygen chamber, a special-ized drug fridge, two sink units, and a wall mounted computer screen to record the dogs treatment information.

In another room there will be the dog bathroom, where the dogs will be washed, brushed, and clipped. Specialist shampoos will be used to treat different skin conditions.

The image my mind is creating is impressive. Even though it's just concrete and wires I can imagine how it will all look once it is finished. I can't wait to come back and see it completed and running at full capacity.

The kitchen/food preparation area has two large storerooms – one for sacks of food, and one for tinned food and bowl storage.

Five different types of dried dog food will be stored in large containers under a long chrome counter, each designed to aid in the recovery of specific illnesses the dogs may suffer from. It will be prepared for each individual animal in the building and placed on trolleys that will then be wheeled around to the kennels. Outside each kennel will be a detailed sign stating who is inside and what is wrong with them, and what medication they are on. A pill tray will be outside each kennel with the medication for that individual animal. The medication, if appropriate, can be mixed with the food, and then the food bowl will be placed in a bracket on the back of the door.

I am shown the different kennels – 8 for intensive care, 20 in the isolation unit, with 11 mother and puppy, and 42 kennels for general holding – 81 in total. Some have partitions that can be raised, so two kennels can become a larger area, for bigger dogs. Also, 29 of the kennels have horizontal, mid-height partitions to allow more dogs to be kept, if required, thus giving a maximum kennel capacity of 110.

Paul points to a drain in the concrete floor next to my pasty flip-flopped feet (which luckily still have ten toes).

"The four inch floor drains (21 in all) had to be specially ordered from the Czech Republic. In Thailand, they only go up to two inches in diameter, which is no good for the volume that will be passing through them – mainly dog hairs, which are caught in special hair traps (that can be removed and cleaned) to save blockage. The 130 kennel drains came from a specialist company in Telford; England called Technik.

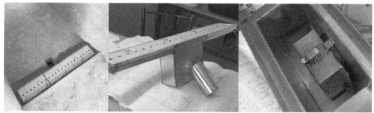

© The specialized kennel drains ordered from Technik in England. It shows the dog hair trap that can be removed and cleaned.

Paul waves a hand around a kennel next to us that is being tiled.

"As well as the 130 kennel drains, 6 specialist examination lights, 1 specialist operating theater light, 1 specialist dental light, 6 fold down examination tables, the 42 guillotine doors, the hydro therapy unit, and smaller items, like the pill trays, were also ordered from Technik.

"Other items such as the kennel gates and fencing, and bespoke stainless steel worktops, sinks, and shelving – basically everything we are not getting from Technik, we have ordered from a specialist, stainless steel making company in Bangkok called KSS."

"As you know, Gill designed the hospital, and through her research, she decided to incorporate guillotine kennel doors, and she decided the kennel drains were also a vital part of the setup. It was through the Dogs Trust architect, Matthew Taylor that the solution was found. He told Gill about Technik the manufacturers of both the guillotine doors and drains. Then, via hundreds of emails between Gill, Matthew, and Technik, and my visit to the UK factory to finalize the designs, a container was packed and loaded aboard a cargo ship, destined for Phuket. The container now rests on our site."

He then points to a pencil mark he has scribbled on a tile.

"Ah, look, here's an example for you," he states. "I walk around and if things aren't up to the standards we expect and require, I write next to it in pencil." He rubs his face. "Sometimes I have caught a worker walking around with a wet cloth rubbing them off instead of fixing the problem, hoping I won't notice. I always notice."

Paul points at gaps between the tiles that should be at least 2 mm.

"If there's no room for the grout, then dirt will get inside. The gaps need to be wide enough to fill with grout."

I look at pencil marks pointing at two tiles that are touching, leaving no room for the grout. If there is no gap in it, it cannot be grouted. The main problem is, even if there is a hairline gap between tiles, bacteria will breed. In the far east, because of the heat and humidity, there is a much faster spread of bacterial growth than in the colder European climate.

"Of course, this also causes another problem. All the columns are either concrete or metal, so on the outside of the tiles, I have written C or M, so when we have to drill into them, we know what's beneath." He looks at a worker who is mixing concrete in a bucket with an electric mixer, as if picking out a culprit.

"The problem is, some walk around thinking the C or M means there's a problem, so they rip the tiles off and redo them. So, the ones that do need replacing they wipe the marks off, and the ones that don't get replaced!"

"Frustrating," I say.

"Tell me about it!"

"There is an interpreter, but the language barrier still causes problems. Sometimes I will see them doing something wrong, and I will try to correct them. If they don't understand I will go and find the interpreter. By the time I return the item in question is gone, or replaced. So they know they are doing it wrong."

Paul points to wires that hang down every few meters along the ceiling.

"These will be speakers that will play relaxing music for the dogs."

I liked that idea.

"We looked into bringing skilled builders and craftsmen, as well as wall and floor tilers from England across for the construction work. However, when you add up the cost of the flights, accommodation, and bringing all their tools and equipment over, it was just way too high. Plus, we like the idea that the work is boosting local jobs, helping the local community and businesses. It's just sometimes it can be a nightmare dealing with the language barrier and different standards."

We walk along a row of kennels.

The kennels have lots of natural light through the clear roof paneling, and a large metal fence that runs down one side of the building, allowing hospital staff to walk around. There will be water points for pressure washing the kennels down. I can also see the specialised drainage system in each kennel.

Paul states all the lights will be LED to save power, and because they give out no heat. In addition, when it is cold there is infra-red heating in the mum and puppy facility to keep the newborns warm. Furthermore, LED lights last ten times longer than conventional bulbs, and due to the massive number that will be in the building, they didn't want someone from maintenance having to spend all their time replacing bulbs.

I was curious about not seeing any solar panels anywhere in Thailand, which I thought would be perfect due to the blazing sun.

Paul states that if they put up enough solar panels to power the complete facility, it would take over twenty years just to break even, and that's without taking into account the maintenance costs, and replacement parts, etc. Also, due to the climate, in twenty years in would most probably need replacing.

We continue walking the bare corridors that have wires hanging everywhere like vines. We check out room after room. Everything has been designed with a specific reason in mind – each is perfectly designed for the task it is required to perform.

I am amazed at the amount of thought that has gone into its construction.

Next to the kennels are the three main utility rooms – the computer server, water, and electricity that sits above a large water storage tank that will feed the whole site. Also there is the large diesel-powered backup generator to keep vital equipment, such as the drug fridges and x-ray and operating equipment working. Power cuts are frequent in the area – just like the rest of Thailand, and most of Asia.

I am fully aware about the power cuts. I have been traveling around Asia for just over a year. The power flickers at least once a day in Thailand. Malaysia is just as bad. I was stuck in a hotel in Siem Reap, Cambodia for almost a week without electricity, and three days without water.

The large diesel-powered backup generator is an absolute necessity.

We end up back at the main entrance after doing a full circuit.

Once complete the building will be the largest and most up-to-date dog hospital in Thailand, and possibly the whole of southeast Asia.

I am in awe of the building and the concept of what it represents – it will truly be impressive once it is completed. The difference it will make to the stray dogs and cats is mind-boggling to comprehend.

The whole way around Paul's enthusiasm for the

building radiated off him like a lighthouse. He is like a proud father watching a child grow before his eyes.

That's the one thing you will notice if you ever get the chance to visit Soi Dog, (which I highly recommend) is that everyone involved is passionate about helping the animals. The energy and love they show is almost palatable. As you walk around the whole facility, everyone is always smiling and happy – positive energy is in abundance, it is invigorating.

It really does amaze me what people can achieve through the power of determination.

Gill and John could have retired and sat on the beach and relaxed, and worried only about them-selves. However, that is not in their nature, (you only have to talk with them for a few minutes to know that they are a remarkable couple). Instead, they followed their hearts, and through their determina-tion and strength of character, (even after life-changing disasters) along with many close friends and long time volunteers and loyal supporters, they followed their hearts and dreams and soon a building that will encapsulate what Soi Dog stands for will be finished and ready to continue their truly inspiring work.

If there was only a handful more people like Gill and John in this world, what a truly different place it would be.

Here is a series of photos showing the progress of the new dog hospital over the months.

© Breaking ground. October 2014.

© Thai customary ceremony to bless the new building. Gill pouring in some foundation concrete over the blessed objects. With John and Paul. November 2014.

© Foundations going down – the 108 support columns. December 2014.

© Foundations complete. Ready for the metal frame. January 2015.

© Main frame started. February 2015.

© Main frame almost complete. March 2015.

© Roof going on. April 2015.

© Paul, (the Project Manager) appearing to be begging for divine intervention to keep them on budget and time. Or he's bragging about a fishing trip? May 2015.

© Gill checking some of the kennels. June 2015.

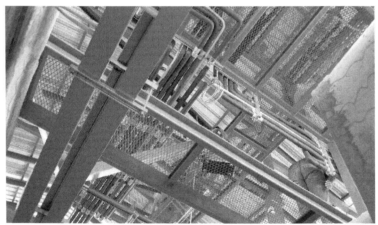

© The electrics starts to worm their way throughout the building. June 2015.

© The unfinished gully around the dog hospital, nick-named the *moat*. July 2015.

© Some of the 110 kennels in the new building. August 2015.

© The tiles start to go up. August 2015.

© The dog hospital, almost complete. August 2015.
Looking from across the dog walking area next to the lake.

This is as far as the build has reached when I completed the book in September 2015. I hope to be back soon to see the building in all its finished glory. (And maybe a second book?)

© The old clinic, soon to be replaced by the new $1,5000,000 dog hospital. (It will still be used for some other purpose).

14

OUT WITH AN ANIMAL WELFARE OFFICER AND GILL

Today is the day I go out with a welfare officer and Gill. To say I am excited is an understatement.

It was almost two weeks after my first visit to Soi Dog (I had been back a couple of times). I spent the time putting the book together in my hotel room at Pensiri House. It was coming together nicely. It was now time to get the information and experience to write another chapter.

I had to communicate with John and Gill via email. So after some back and forth correspondence it was arranged for me to go out with a welfare officer called Sanae. The problem is, he doesn't speak English, and my Thai is a little rusty... who am I kidding; I don't know a single word of Thai. So it was arranged that Gill would be joining us. I was honored when I found out I would be spending some time with one of the co-founders.

It turns out that some of the dogs recognize the white Soi Dog truck's logo, so when the truck approaches the dog's bolt. So there are little pockets where the welfare officers have yet to catch the animals and get them sterilized.

So Gill would head out first with her car, with me in the back (scribbling notes) and Sanae in the front with a container filled with the tranquilizer chemicals and the parts for the darts, and the four-foot long blow dart tube over his shoulder.

Behind us another officer followed at a distance in a Soi Dog truck, so as not to spook the animals.

The plan was the dogs wouldn't recognize Gill's car, so we could simply pull up next to them and dart them.

Easy-peasy I thought. I would be back at the Guest Hut in no time for a cuppa tea. After all, as I sit in the hut, the trucks arrive one after the other filled with dogs. How hard can it be?

Easy is the last word I would use to describe the process of catching a dog.

We left Soi Dog and headed out down the long winding road.

Up front, Sanae spent the time putting the darts together. His movements were of a person that has performed the task a thousand times before – he was quick and efficient.

The dart is about nine inches long and is made up of three parts, and the tranquilizing liquid. First the section where the chemical is held, which is attached to another tube the same size that is pumped with air, to make a compressed chamber. The needle has a release mechanism on it, so as the dart hits the dog, the act of going in activates a switch that releases the compressed air that plunges the injection and forces the tranquilizer into the animal.

Sanae had the container open on his lap, and with a special device he was screwing a needle onto the dart after he filled it with chemicals. He then pumped the compressed air chamber and attached the bright orange tail, that would stabilize it in flight, and also make it easy to find in the undergrowth when it drops off. It also made a plug in the dart tube, so he could blow it out at a velocity powerful enough to cover an impressive distance.

I wondered if the colour orange was just a coincidence, since it is the same colour as the Soi Dog logo?

Gill pointed out that blow darts are used because they are cheaper, and required no license, unlike a gun or rifle. It is also easier to learn to use one.

The needles are Dutch and are ordered specially from a company in Europe.

When I asked why from so far away, Gill replied, "Because they are the best we can find; well-made and sturdy. They last longer."

Each dart can be used numerous times.

The problem is, Gill states, "The instant the needle goes in the dog runs off. We then have to chase after it, until the chemicals take effect. Sometimes the needle drops right out. Sometimes the dog runs off with it. On numerous occasions, we lose darts because we can't find the dog. It simply runs off too far away and falls asleep. It then wakes up, pulls the dart out, and carries on as if nothing has happened."

We turn onto the Sirinat National Park. The park was established in 1981. It is a green belt of land that kisses the beach and runs up into the mountains behind. It covers thirty-five square miles. Twenty-six square miles are marine (which protects the coral reefs that are seven hundred meters off shore), with a further nine square miles of land. It covers four beaches: Hat Nai Thon, Hat Nai Yang, Hat Mai Khao, and Hat Sai Kaeo. We were in the Hat Nai Yang section.

Nai Yang is the beach where we are staying. Only the day before Gary and I had walked down this end of the beach and walked through the park. We noticed a lot of skittish stray dogs. Along one section, opposite the beach, over the road, is a long strip of street venders. They create a lot of trash.

There are two square miles of forest along the beach, which is the area we are now entering.

The area around the beach has trees spaced evenly, which helps to buffer the wind pouring off the Andaman Sea. Behind, over the road, the trees are thicker, and it becomes a forest; the whole area is awash in an impenetrable wall of vibrant trees. Tree species include common ironwood, tulip tree, tropical almond, white barringtonia, cajeput tree, Alexandrian laurel, screwpine, ashoka tree, black plum, elephant apple and morning glory.

I was about to become very familiar with some of the flora, along with red ants that decide to chew on my feet.

Gill drives down the main road, along the sea front. Beach to the right, with a strip of trees, and the forest to our left.

It's just after 1 pm and about 35°C, which feels like 45 with the added humidity.

We pull into an open grass car park that has towering trees dotted around with vines hanging from their branches, making it look like the tree was growing a beard. We drove through toward some holiday bungalows that back onto an inlet.

Slowly, the car drives around, as we check every section. This is where the dogs have been spotted.

I'm surprised when I'm told the animal welfare officers know every dog they have caught and have sterilized. The instant they see a dog; they know if it's new to the area. Also, every animal that has been neutered and inoculated has a small tattoo in one ear.

We drive right around the large area. Then, to one side, just in view is three puppies that are probably just a few months old. Gill pulls the car over next to an empty holiday bungalow.

Sanae reaches around his seat looking for something next to me.

Gill points out he's putting a shirt over his Soi Dog T-shirt, because like the orange logo on the van, the dogs recognize them.

With a grey shirt on, covering up his top, Sanae collects the three darts he has put together and gets out, taking the four-foot blow dart tube with him.

Sanae slowly walks toward the dogs that are laid down, rolling on the ground.

© Sanae slowly walking towards the dogs with the jungle ahead.

However, the instant the dogs see him they bolt into the thick jungle. Sanae gave chase, but was back in a few minutes.

Gill and I waited back in the car. If too many of us get out at once, the dog's race off straight away.

Sanae crouched, ready for the animals to come back.

Gill decided to turn the car around. The problem is, we were stuck – the front tires have sunk in the soft, dusty earth. I got out and pushed us free.

I am now covered in a thin layer of sweat.

While this was going on, Sanae was waiting patiently for the puppies to return. He was hidden in the bushes.

Gill climbed from the car and watched Sanae in the distance. You could tell she wished she could take a more active part, but due to her two prosthetic legs, she couldn't.

It turned out, after twenty minutes waiting, the dogs had run farther into the jungle. We needed to change location.

© Gill watching Sanae. You can just see him hiding in the top right-hand corner.

We got back into the car, and Gill drove us back the way we came, to a side road that led around the back of the bungalows we were just beside, on the other side of the deep inlet.

I found out where all the taxis are hiding. The small lane led to a huge car park that was filled with at least fifty taxis and minibuses. In one corner, is a street vendor stall set up, all in the open.

Gill went to speak with the owners – she is not fluent in Thai but can get by.

It turns out; there are about ten regular dogs that hang around the area, scavenging.

About fifteen taxi drivers hung around the tables. Some were gambling, which is illegal in Thailand. No wonder they all looked nervous when we first walked over. When they found out we are from Soi Dog, they all relaxed a little.

The outside restaurant is right up in the corner of the car park, with thick jungle to one side.

We hear a shout. Sanae has darted a dog. He races into the trees. Gill is quickly on his heels.

I stand back and watch, not sure of what I'm supposed to do?

© Gill chatting with the vendor lady.

Sanae returns and with hand signals states I should be following Gill.

I find a section that is passable and head in.

In my bag, in the car, is a set of trainers. In the rush and excitement, I forgot to put them on. At present, I am wearing flip-flops, not the best foot-wear to walk through the jungle with.

I have never walked in a real jungle before, just scraps of trees here and there in Malaysia and Cambodia that have paths leading through them. However, this was a real jungle.

Within seconds, I felt a sting race up my body, as if Sanae had shot a dart into my leg. I look down. There is a big red ant with its mandibles clamped into my flesh. With a slap that could crack lumber, I turned it into a smear.

I look up, and Gill is just visible through the undergrowth. The trees thinned out a little and open up into a clearing.

This is the part where the dog has run off after being darted, and we now have to find it.

© Gill up ahead as the trees open up into a clearing.

Gill is scanning everywhere, in case the brown dog is lying down.

How anyone could find a motionless dog in the undergrowth, in such a large area is mind-boggling.

I take one side of the clearing, scanning the jungle floor.

There is a feeling of life present all around; everything seems to be moving. Everything apart from a dog.

The sound of insects is almost deafening. Chirping, beeping, ringing and buzzing – it is a cacophony of sound.

I squash another red ant that has bitten my little toe. It feels like a quick, sharp electrical jolt, that makes your whole-body jump. Luckily, apart from the initial bite hurting like hell, there is no lingering effect – no agonizing pain. No swelling of limbs. No blood dripping from my eye sockets. So all is good.

I make a mental note: Never, ever wear flip-flops into a jungle again!

As I think that, scampering over the tip of my left flip-flop – mere millimeters away from my toes – is a ten inch black armored millipede on hundreds of undulating legs. They don't bite and have no sting or pincers, but I am told they emit a compound that can severely burn or blister skin if they touch you. I quickly pull my foot away as a shiver runs down my spine.

I look up.

Gill is nowhere to be seen.

Ah!

I forget about the dog and start looking for Gill. I have absolutely no sense of direction. Turn me around twice and I'm lost.

I start checking for movement.

Nothing.

I head towards where I think I saw Gill last.

Still nothing.

A few minutes have passed, and you would be amazed at the amount that can rush through your brain in a couple of minutes.

I have seen numerous National Geographic shows where people get lost mere miles from civilization. How, even though the jungle is full of food, they starve to death, or die of dehydration. I have mental images of newspaper headlines:

AUTHOR DIES THREE HUNDRED
METERS FROM A BUSY CAR PARK

HUNT FOR MISSING
AUTHOR: DAY FIVE

I am becoming frantic.

Is that people I hear? It's hard to tell through the sound of the insects.

When you watch wildlife documentaries and there're clips in a jungle with the buzzing insects and chattering birds, it really doesn't do it justice. One creature is making a sound that is painful and sounds like a high-pitched whining. It physically hurts my ears.

It shows just how easy it is to get lost. And how completely unprepared we are when it happens. I have a wallet on me, (you don't see many shops in the jungle), and a small plastic bottle, which has about three warm gulps of water left in it. I am wearing just shorts, a tee-shirt, and flip-flops. I am completely unprepared for jungle survival.

I have no idea how long I have been wandering in circles. Minutes, hours? When suddenly Sanae is stood right in front of me. I have no idea where he came from, or how he managed to get so close without me even noticing.

I really need to get some survival skills sorted out. Can you learn a sense of direction, or do you have to be born with it?

He waves a hand for me to follow him. I do.

It turns out, I was only about a hundred meters from the car park and everyone.

I hide my relief. Visions of me being eaten alive by ants fade.

Back to dog catching.

I missed them finding the dog and putting it in a truck. It was already on the way back to Soi Dog. Not to worry, there's another group of animals in behind the car park.

Gill spots some more dogs. Sanae phones the truck to get them to bring it around.

© Gill and Sanae, with another animal welfare officer, spotting a black dog in the distance.

Sanae races off with his blow dart. I stay back near the people in the car park, who are playing cards.

In the distance, I can see Sanae crouching, readying to fire a dart.

Sanae doesn't get a chance to fire.

This is the problem with catching the dogs; no two days are ever the same. There are no definite ways of doing it. Some days are good, others are bad.

We have been out for over three hours, and the four of us have caught just one dog.

© Sanae crouching, blow dart ready.

I say the four of us, I'm simply watching, getting lost, and being bitten to death. I had been bitten on the back of the legs, by mosquitoes in the jungle, so many times that if a blind person ran a hand over my calves, they would think they were reading a novel.

We all get back into the car and head down the road. There is another animal welfare officer in our car, sat in the back with me, he has joined us from the truck.

Down the road is a turnoff where trash is illegally dumped. It is wet, boggy, dirty, and very smelly. The dogs scavenge through the rubbish, looking for food. They don't show you places like this in the travel brochures. It's sad that this mess is right inside a national park.

There are dog's mere meters away right outside the car, just on the turning into the dumping area. However, if Sanae opens a door, they will scarper. He tries to shoot them from the car, through a lowered window.

He hits one, and it runs off into the jungle with a

loud yelping sound trailing behind.

Gill drives the car in as far as she can without damaging the underside on the uneven ground.

Gill and I wait among the trash and smell, as Sanae and another animal welfare officer from Soi Dog race after the darted dog. They quickly vanish into the thick jungle undergrowth with a lot of crashing and snapping of branches.

© Sanae aiming out of the window at a black dog.

It starts to patter with rain.

Gill and I move to stand under a tree.

"This is the bit I miss the most," Gill states. "I used to love the chase, running after them, making sure they are safe." She looks down at her legs. "Of course, I can't any more."

I think about almost getting lost, and bitten by angry ants that feel like a jolt of lightning.

"Has anyone ever been hurt, chasing after them?" I quickly add, "apart from yourself, that is."

"One catcher came face to face with a cobra, that was fully hooded and ready to strike, mere feet away. That was a close call," she says.

© Gill and Sanae next to the illegal dumping ground. Sanae is about to race after the darted dog.

What? I was so preoccupied with being lost, only moments ago; I had no idea there were poisonous snakes in the area.

After a few minutes of waiting in silence Gill announced, "John and I used to do it alone at one point, when we first started." She has a faraway look in her eyes.

"John could shoot the dart farther than me, but I was better at waiting. I could sit for ages in one place, until the dogs forgot I was there, and ambled back."

There was a call from the jungle. Sanae has found the darted dog. He appeared with his helper and between them; they carried the large black, unconscious dog.

With a call on his phone, Sanae got the Soi Dog truck to drive up into the dumping area, so he could load the dog onboard.

Gill and I climb back into her car and start to

head back to Soi Dog.

© Sanae putting the darted dog into the Soi Dog truck.

"So, do you want to see the complete process?" Gill Asks. "Do you want to see the sterilization operation?"

"Yes please," I say.

THE STERILIZATION OPERATION

I had been out with Gill and Sanae for almost three hours, and I needed to use the toilet. So while the tranquilized black dog was unloaded into the Sterilization Clinic, I rushed to the toilet in the cat building.

I was only gone a few minutes, and when I arrived, Gill was waiting.

"Quick, he has already gone into surgery!"

I was informed the large animal was already coming around from the dart, so rather than tranquilize it again; they took it straight into the operating room.

Normally, the dog would be shaved in another section of the clinic, beside the main gate, as they enter. However, because it needed to be attached to the general anesthetic machine to keep it sedated, and to regulate its breathing, it was already in the main operating room.

I entered to the sight of the large black dog on the floor, as it was being prepared to be lifted onto the metal table, which had two long pillows to keep the animal in position.

There are three operating tables in the room.

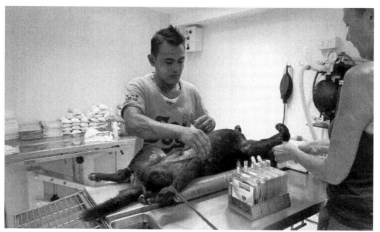

© The dog is stabilized, and Kae, the vets assistant, is preparing to shave the area ready for the operation.

Kae, the vet's assistant, starts to shave the skin over the animal's groin, penis sheath (prepuce) and scrotum with a very sharp blade. You can tell he has done it thousands of times before. He then wipes the area down with two different types of antiseptic – a clear solution, and then a yellow one. By the time the vet arrives, the dog is all prepped and ready.

The sedative used contains a pain-relief drug which reduces pain during and after the surgery. Also, the sedative action results in lower amounts of anesthetic drugs being needed to keep the animal asleep.

The drugs also reduce the production of saliva and airway secretions; this reduces the amount the dog drools, and the risk that saliva and respiratory secretions may be inhaled into the lungs during surgery. It also improves blood pressure and airway dilation – making it easier for the animal to breathe.

The general anesthesia is achieved by giving the dog an intravenous injection of an anesthetic drug – which it received from the blow dart – which is then followed up with and maintained using an anesthetic inhalational gas. The dog has a tube inserted down its throat during the surgery to facilitate the administration of the anesthetic gas.

Doctor Eed arrives in blue scrubs with a green hairnet. Without hesitation, or fuss, she is passed a bundle by Kae.

The bundle is a clean bed sheet cut up, with the implements required for each sterilization. Each bundle contains five items: four clamps, a pair of scissors, and a scalpel.

With the area all shaved and disinfected, Dr. Eed starts.

Sterilizing (or otherwise known as neutering in the case of male dogs), is the surgical removal of a male dog's testicles. During the quick procedure, each of the dog's testes and testicular epididymi are removed along with sections of the dog's testicular blood vessels and spermatic ducts.

Dr. Eed lays out the implements on a white cloth, then she uses the strip of material they were wrapped in, after she cut a hole in it, to place over the area, she is about to operate on.

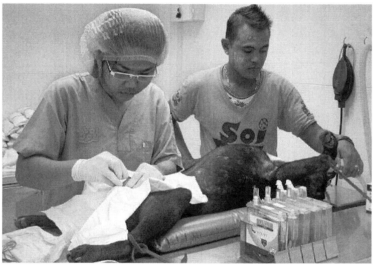

© Doctor Eed performing the operation, with Kae checking the animals breathing.

She makes a swift, controlled incision with the scalpel into the skin just ahead of the animal's scrotal sac, on the midline of the animal.

Kae keeps an eye on the dog's breathing.

Through the cut that looks to be about two inches long, Dr. Eed then removes the testicals, pulling them both out of the same hole, one at a time. The long ductus deferens (that joins the testicals to the body) are pulled right out, extending a good six or seven inches outside of the scrotal sack. Using two clips, she clamps each one, stopping the blood flow.

As I watch the procedure, Gill is talking me through it. She is amazed that I'm not squirming. She states that she finds about ninety-five percent of men can't watch the operation. For some reason, watching the nuts getting cutoff effects them in strange ways – being sick, fainting, or just having to get out of the room, she says she has seen it all. However, it has no effect on me at all – I am intrigued and taking it all in to be able to put it into words.

On the table in front of Dr. Eed is a case that has five different types of *Catgut* sutures in. (it looks like thin cotton that you would sow with).

Catgut suture is a type of surgical suture that is naturally degraded by the body's own proteolytic enzymes. Absorption is complete by ninety days, and full tensile strength remains for at least seven days. This eventual disintegration makes it perfect for use with stray dogs, where they are released within hours or days, and the suture will not be able to be manually removed. It simply degrades and falls away.

Catguts, I would like to point out, even though it is called cat guts, is made by twisting together strands of purified collagen taken from the small intestine of healthy cattle, sheep, or goats, even from beef tendon. No cats are harmed in its making.

She uses some suture to tie around each of the long ductus deferens sections. Then she clamps near each suture, so when she cuts the testicals away, they will not bleed.

With two swipes of the scalpel, the dog has been

sterilized. The two purple, oval sacks rest on the white cloth, with a clamp on each one.

Dr. Eed then sows up the incision.

© The Soi Dog vets: (From left to right) Dr. Katherine, Dr. Jennifer, Dr. Eed, Dr. Su, Dr. Pam, and Dr. Eugene.

Duan, a young female assistant has replaced Kae, and she is getting a disinfected plaster ready, which will rest over the stitches. As Dr. Eed stands aside, Duan steps in and lays the white plaster over the cut. She then grabs the animal and lifts it from the table and takes it out and places it on a black padded mat, until the dog comes around, then it is checked over, and moved to the kennels for the night. The next day it will be taken back to the location it was removed from if fully recovered.

The reason for returning the animal to the same location is simple; it has already set up its territory, so it can be replaced, and once the other animals in the area have also been sterilized; the zone will be under control, and the population will slowly decline.

Dogs that live around built-up areas are known by the shop owners, and some are even fed by them, so they are returned. However, if they need extra treatment, that keeps them away from their territory for too long, they need to be kept at Soi Dog until a new home can be found.

I hope you have enjoyed my tour, and I hope you visit the links provided in the book, to be able to get a better understanding of the amazing work carried out by the Soi Dog Foundation.

If you ever get chance to visit Phuket, Thailand, I highly recommend spending the day at Soi Dog – you, and your family will love it.

Also, why not consider sponsoring one of the many animals at Soi Dog?

www.soidog.org/en/sponsor-a-
dog-or-cat/Default.aspx

15

VOLUNTEERING IN RUN A4

So far, I have been taken on tours of different buildings, I've been out with Gill and a welfare officer, seen all the volunteers walking the dogs, sat with (and under a pile of) the cats for endless hours, (Rolex and Raisin are my favorites). I have followed Inga around to listen to her explain how the foundation works to visitors (twice – once a VIP tour around areas most visitors never walk through), and I have sat in the guest hut for hours on end chatting with and listening to the other volunteers who have arrived from all around the world, giving up their time and energy for the betterment of the animals.

From my location in the guest hut I have witnessed volunteers walking around the lake hundreds of times, as I sit making notes and gulping cold water to stay hydrated.

Now it was my time to volunteer and get my

own dog run to look after – experience firsthand what hundreds of others volunteers have achieved – and why they keep coming back.

First, I have the weekend to relax. Soi Dog is closed on the weekends, to give the Burmese employees, and the long-term volunteers a break, and the animals a rest.

DAY ONE VOLUNTEERING

Before I know it, it is Monday morning and the alarm clock on my mobile phone announces it is time to crawl out of bed. I might of mentioned I'm not a morning person – that is a gross understatement. My body refuses to function with any form of coordination until at least midday.

I imagine other volunteers in the hotel going through the same routine as I am – going toilet, showering, shaving (not the women – well, maybe some of them) getting dressed, gulping down coffee, brushing my teeth and grabbing my backpack before heading out the sliding patio door.

The Soi Dog truck arrives at 8:45 am to scoop up the zombiefied volunteers, who sway slightly as they stand waiting in the heat that has already made the mercury rise into the mid-twenties.

As I head over from Pensiri House's new building, I see bright, enthusiastic new faces.

You can tell who has been here for a few days or weeks (or have volunteered before), they are more relaxed and chat among themselves – about their weekend, and the dogs at Soi Dog, or ones they see at the beach, whereas the newbie's stand looking nervous, not quite sure of what to expect.

The new volunteers also look too clean. They wear smart clothes, perfect hair and makeup, not knowing what awaits them. When you see them on the second morning, they are more casual, with wrinkled, older clothing, with natural hair (normally, a hat of some kind rammed down to keep their hair in place) with hardly any makeup. They have realized no one cares what they look like, it's all about the animals.

There's a chorus of nervous "Hellos" and "Where are you from?" and "Is this your first time?" kind of questions. I pick up English, German, American, and Australian accents.

Today, it turns out Pond (the normal Thai driver) is busy, so Darren (a long-time volunteer) is our designated chauffeur. He told those who were at Soi Dog on Friday that he would be late. I wasn't there on Friday; I was crouched over my laptop, writing. So as 8:45 comes and goes, people start mulling around, nervous.

One new volunteer, a young woman who was born in Hong Kong, but now lives in Perth Australia, is the only one that is glad Pond is late, because the breakfast she ordered still hasn't arrived. She sits nervously with her boyfriend, hoping she will have time to eat her food. She also has a large cardboard box, and a smaller sturdy material bag that is filled with drugs and medical supplies for the clinic that she is donating. She is a veterinarian student, and she is here to volunteer for two days at the clinic.

Then at 9 am small white Soi Dog car arrives.

No way are we all getting in that, I think to myself.

Four new volunteers get in, and the driver said he would be back to pick up the rest. It is at least twenty minutes each way to Soi Dog, and there are enough people for two more trips. Plus, as the car drives off, more volunteers start to arrive.

"Yeah, we were told Pond was away, so the truck would be late today," Sabina said. "It's great; we got a sleep-in." Behind her is her partner Brad. Brad is a mountain of a man – he looks like he could lift a car up with one hand. However, when he is around the dogs, he becomes a gentle giant.

Sabina Archibald who is twenty-seven, and Brad Brinkworth, who is thirty-six have been volunteering at the foundation the whole previous week – I have seen and chatted with them on numerous occasions.

They are a friendly, upbeat, energetic couple from Margaret River, Western Australia. They own a rental business in a stunning district, with rivers and mountains and forests, and Brad works security at a large mining complex.

Sabina is by far the most passionate, caring volunteer I have witnessed in my many weeks at Soi Dog. She's like a supernova pouring out positive vibes.

"We would love to take them all home with us," she said, referring to the dogs in the A1 Run. I believe her. In fact, they talk about starting a GoFundMe page, or a Kickstarter page, to help raise money to be able to send some of the dogs in Run A1 to Australia.

A couple of other volunteers who were there on Friday start to arrive, knowing the truck would be late.

Hannah and Helen arrive.

Hannah Coffey is twenty-three and from Gloucestershire, England. Helen Feeney is thirty-six and from Preston, England.

The Pensiri House shop opens at 9 am, so I purchased an ice-cold coffee in a can, and a packet of chicken flavor peanuts (breakfast of champions). I sit down at a concrete patio set outside the shop watching the volunteers interact.

The new volunteers group together.

We are expecting the car, but instead the normal large truck arrives with Darren driving. The twelve of us pile in – four in the air-conditioned cab, and eight in the back. There is a row of seats, one to each side of the metal caged canopy. I let everyone climb inside so I balance on the last inch of seating, with one cheek levitating over the gap.

The conversations cover what everyone was doing over the weekend. What restaurants did they go to? Were they any good? How much was the food? Did they go and feed the stray dogs at the end of the beach? Some discussed how their dogs behaved in their runs the week before.

Sabina arranges for someone else to continue feeding the stray dogs she has befriended on the beach.

Then the new volunteers started to join in as they were asked questions. Where are you from? How long are you here for? Are you a vet, or will you be helping in the runs? How did you hear about Soi Dog? Are you on your own?

Those that are on their own make little groups that start to hang around together at night – going out for meals or drinks or walks to the local market.

I lean sideways looking out the back grated doors, and listen to everyone's conversations. I find I only talk when someone asks me a question or talks to me first – I'm quite shy.

Mostly, I just listen.

The truck heads past numerous hotels and guesthouses, snaking its way along winding roads, then out past Phuket's airport and then onto the wide, main motorway.

No matter how many times I travel this route the scenery still captivates me. So much greenery – towering palm trees and waterlogged fields full of buffalo's with their huge arching horns that look like a really bad 80s parted haircut.

The truck turns down the lane leading to Soi Dog. A sign announces its 2.9 km away. I think they have changed it, I'm sure it used to say 500 meters? The new sign is more accurate – the first day I arrived in a taxi and got 500 meters down the road; we looked around in confusion when it was nowhere in sight.

Hotels are replaced by private homes. Every house is individual. Some are grand and impressive, looking like stately mansions, surrounded by raked gravel, manicured lawns and clipped hedges; others are wooden huts built on stilts, with swinging hammocks and chickens scratching at the baked dusty earth.

There are dogs on the road, barking as we pass. Some have collars on, but most don't; they all look healthy and well fed. There's one small white poodle by a junction that's always sat watching the road.

We arrive at Soi Dog. The excitement rises in the truck. Some of the volunteers have been waiting and saving for years to come visit and help out at the foundation.

We pile out of the truck and herd into the guest hut.

Diana is waiting to welcome the newbies.

Those that already have runs collect their bags off the hooks and start to organize themselves for a day of dog walking and interaction.

Bags are dropped onto the two large tables as everyone fills their water bottles or grab tea or coffee. Conversations explode as people from the truck's cab catch up with those who were sat in the back.

Diana gathers the new volunteers together, explaining how the system works. (Long time volunteer Diana and Mark Van De Wall's story is covered in detail in chapter 25).

Even though I have been coming to Soi Dogs complex on and off for almost seven weeks, and know how everything is organized and run, and could probably walk around and give the tour myself, I am here to experience what the volunteers go through, so I sit and listen along with them.

The first day consists of lots of sitting and listening. A form to fill out, videos to watch and instructions to follow. If you are here for just a few hours or a day, you don't get assigned your own run, but after watching the safety videos you can walk the dogs from the OAP, Small, Or Hotel runs. They don't want to put a person into a main run if they are not staying, so as not to confuse the animals.

As it turns out, our guide for the tour is Darren, not Diana. I've not been on a tour with Darren yet; I'm intrigued as to what his style will be. (Long time volunteer Darren and Deb Benbrook's story is covered in detail in chapter 24).

We gather around Darren as he starts our tour.

As well as myself, there's Meghan Durno, who's is twenty-three and from Glasgow, Scotland. She has just finished her veterinary nurse's course, and wants to help out. Meghan is planning on staying for about a month.

There is also Lexx Bartlett, who is twenty-two and from England.

A young German female in her mid-twenties, who is very shy called, Sina, and who (over the coming days) had the worse case of mosquito bites I have ever seen – she was pickled in them. (It was never determined if it was bites or a reaction to something?)

Also a female in her late twenties who was born in Hong Kong but lives in Australia (she had time to finish her breakfast). I missed catching her name.

There is also a male Chinese teenager who is here just for the day, (he is very touchy-feely and is the first to stroke or hug every dog we come across), and two mid-thirties women who are also here just for the day who were here already when we arrived.

Together we gather around as Darren explains the running of Soi Dog.

I have already explained a tour in one of the previous chapters, so I don't want to be repetitive and bore you.

However, I did learn a few new things from

Darren – I'm not saying he is a better tour guide than Inga, they just both have different styles.

I learned there is a flight company called Nok Air, which flies the dogs saved from the dog meat trade from Bangkok to Phuket for Soi Dog for free.

Also, as we walked past the old clinic, soon to be replaced by the new dog hospital, we saw a street dog that has just been taken out into the yard. The poor thing was in bad shape, and it was in the fenced in area waiting to be looked at by a vet. As we passed, its back legs shook, and the poor thing had a bad case of diarrhea. A brown spray shot across the concrete yard.

Behind me I heard a female voice say, "Tell me about it, I know just how it feels – Thai food has the same effect on me!"

After about half an hour, we are back in the guest hut. Just as we settle down to watch some instruction videos, Gill arrives and pulls up in her car. She gets out and retrieves some objects from the back seat. One is a framed photo of a dog, another is a sign.

A Burmese staff member is asked if he can hang them up.

It turns out the guest hut has been renamed Dominic's Place. A new sign goes on the hut outside, and a photo of an old grey, happy looking dog, with a bandana around his neck is hung next to the white board.

Dominic was at Soi Dog from 2005 to 2015 then he was adopted by a lady from Canada who had volunteered at the shelter, and had fallen in love with Dominic. Sadly, after only a few months in

Canada, he passed away. Dominic was the only dog who had free run of the compound. He used to socialize with the volunteers in the guest hut. He is a character who will never be forgotten, and is part of Soi Dog's history. The renamed hut and his framed photo are testament to how he touched people's hearts.

© Dominic's photo hung up in the guest hut (Dominic's Place).

Lunchtime has arrived. Our food, that we ordered in the morning, turns up, and we sit around chatting while consuming our rice or noodles. I have chicken fried rice. A small sachet of fish/chili sauce come with it. It is covered in oil that makes in slippery. It takes me a good couple of minutes to get into it.

It starts to pour down, and when it rains here, it lashes down. There is no slow build up, or gentle mist – one minute it is overcast, the next, torrential rain; the sort that pits the earth and cause's flash floods, accompanied by deep bass thunder and flashing lightning.

The mood changes, because the volunteers know they can't walk the dogs in the rain.

Lunchtime comes and goes, but everyone hangs around in Dominic's Place out of the downpour.

I, however, have things I can do. I get soaked walking to the offices. Here Paul has a table. I sit with Paul going through hundreds of photos of the dog hospital build on his laptop, looking for photos to use for the book. I write down about eighty or so I like, and Paul passes the list onto Raymond Gerritsen, who created a Drop Box for me with the images in.

Because of the rain I then go and sit with the cats in Run 1 and 2 for an hour or so.

© I'm enjoying a hug with Nai Yang in Cat Run 1.

Before I know it, the first day is over, and we all meet back in the guest hut (Dominic's Place) to wait for the truck to drive us back to Pensiri.

DAY TWO VOLUNTEERING

It is easier getting up for the second day, because staying outside for most of the day yesterday, in the heat, sapped my strength, and I found it easy to fall asleep.

I wander over to where we are picked up. Before long, I am on the same seat bouncing over potholes and metal grates as we head to Soi Dog.

Today is different. Today I have my own dog run and animals to walk.

As soon as we unload from the truck I look up at the white board and find I have been paired off with Maria in Run A4.

Maria Raja is from Stockport, England. She is thirty-seven and married with two children, and is studying counseling and Psychotherapy.

I joked at one point asking if she was psychoanalyzing me. She just smiled.

Maria has left behind her husband of fifteen years, and her thirteen and fifteen-year-old boys to volunteer at Soi Dog for three weeks.

As some of the others settle down to relax before heading to their runs, Maria wants to get started as soon as possible. She grabs the bright yellow waterproof bag for A4, and we head straight over.

Each run has its own bag. Each bag contains 3 leads, a dog brush, and a book with the names and stories (if known) of each of the dogs in the particular run.

There are eight main runs A1, 2, 3, and 4, and also B1, 2, 3, and 4. Each run has up to twenty dogs. At present there are just over 400 dogs at Soi Dog in Phuket.

© B4 Run. Showing the size and shape of the run. Taken from the tower.

There are sixteen dogs in *our* run – ten males, and six females. The males are: Na Tong, Boyce, Dr. Who, Dickenson, Ginger, Gita, Kamari, Silvan, Sten, and Tumi. The females are: Apple, Emi, Lindsey, Misha, Trin, and Wawa.

I remember looking through the A4 Runs folder. Each dog has its own page, with a photo and a section with details about the animal's character. For example, are they shy or boisterous, or will they keep to themselves or jump up at you?

Na Tong's sheet says:

NAME: Na Tong (male)
DOB: 2008

- Do not lift him up when he escapes, etc.

- Tends to nip you, and jump on you.

- Walk him first, he will then calm down.

I also remember reading the five main instructions for all the volunteers working in the runs.

1. Stand in front of the run, wait for the dogs to calm down.

2. Only open the gate when no one else is opening their gate into their run or one of the main entrance gates.

3. When you enter the run, just keep walking. Do NOT forget to CLOSE the gate when you enter or leave the run.

4. Once inside, walk around. Do not give the dogs any attention yet. Wait for them to calm down.

5. Once everyone is calm, you can sit next to a dog and socialize with him or her. Or, take one for a walk.

As we head over, Maria explains about the pecking order, starting with the alpha male, then female. Then all the other dogs have a position on the list, as to how they treat each other, because they are housed in groups and the animals have a pack mentality.

We enter the main gate, with A runs to the left and B runs to the right, and the enrichment area (where you can take individual dogs and let them off the lead and play with them) straight ahead.

© Main gate into the A and B Runs and Enrichment Area.

We head through another gate, which leads to our A4 run. All the dogs are jumping up at the fence when they recognize Maria, knowing they are about to get walked. Some are barking, while others are yelping or whining.

Maria enters first, while using her legs to stop the excited dogs from pushing out past her into the enclosed space.

I enter, and I am instantly engulfed by dogs – jumping up, racing around me, licking, nipping, bashing into me.

Some of the quieter dogs, ones lower down the ranks sit or circle just out of reach – it's not their place to welcome new people.

Na Tong is the alpha male, and he is sponsored by Soozie Hall, a friend of mine in England. (More about Soozie sponsoring Na Tong in chapter 22). I became friends with Soozie through Facebook interactions, and I was surprised that after she heard I was writing a book about Soi Dog, she went to their website, and the next minute she was sponsoring Na Tong.

© Run A4 (with 16 dogs – mainly around the gate).

Here I was, being nipped at by Na Tong because he is the alpha male, and he was letting me know that he had better be the first dog walked today.

Maria looped her lead around Na Tong and after a few missed attempts, I managed to lasso Apple – the alpha female, who is so broad shouldered; she's bigger than most of the males in the run.

With the two alpha's heading out the gate, the run quietens down considerably.

One at a time, we exit the different gates. Each gate is there in case a dog escapes – to keep them from racing off – so there're a few to exit through.

Once free of the runs, we head toward the large artificial lake.

There are no other walkers out yet, just us, so we have the lake to ourselves. I can see the others still in the guest hut, finishing their coffee.

© Maria in Run A4, with Ginger, Dr. Who, and Wawa.

We space out to let the dogs enjoy their walk. They spend most of their time in with other dogs, so this is their time. They sniff and pee their way around the lake. I never realized dogs have such big bladders.

At intervals, there are water bowls; little bone-shaped plastic bag dispensers for the dog waste, and bins to put it in. Also concrete benches in case the volunteers need a rest, or in case the dogs do, and we have somewhere to sit.

The second dog I walked is Ginger, a large rowdy male. Apparently, he was bullied by another dog when he was younger, and he has never forgotten, especially now he's large and powerful. The dog that picked on him is in another run, and she is called Gypsy.

© My first experience of walking a dog at Soi Dog. This is Apple, the alpha female in run A4.

Just my luck, Brad is just behind me walking the white dog Gypsy.

As soon as Ginger notices her, he goes crazy, raising up on his hind legs and twisting and turning to get off the collar. I end up almost having to drag Ginger around the lake – he is so hell-bent on getting to Gypsy for a bit of payback.

By the time I get Ginger back in the run my shoulder feels like it has been dislocated.

Maria took Ginger out for his second lap later when he had calmed down.

I worked my way through the sixteen dogs in run A4, helping Maria, who knows the individual animals better.

© Ginger walking around the lake. Better behaved with no Gypsy in sight.

Next is Lindsey, a small, energetic dog. Then Trin, a three-legged dog that kind of walks with her front legs and hops with her one rear leg. She gets tired easily, and I stop often. Then the twins, Emi and Yumi – Maria and I take one each – brother and sister. Then I take a very active, loving black dog out, who is always after attention, and who has a very memorable name he's called Dr. Who.

I am covered in muddy paw prints from when they jump up whenever I enter the run. My flip-flop feet are kedged in mud and grit. In their excitement, the amount of times they step on your feet is unbelievable. Also, when you walk the dogs around the lake, they pee, then scratch at the ground, rubbing their scent in. The problem is, I have never seen a dog do this before, so when Apple took her first pee, she scratched at the ground and completely covered me in a spray of mud and grit. You also have to constantly keep an eye on the dog you are walking, because if you are stood in the wrong place, you will get covered in sprayed mud, over and over.

I walk the dogs one after another from 9:15 am until 12 pm.

I head back to the guest hut for lunch. First, I pop into the toilet that has an attached hose on the wall – I used it to wash the mud off my legs, feet, and arms.

Feeling clean, I sit down to a lunch of fried rice and chicken – a winning recipe, in my opinion, (plus another fight getting into the sauce).

Now I know why the volunteers are a little quiet while they eat lunch – they are exhausted from walking around the lake, playing with the dogs in the run, and the heat and humidity. Today it is 32 degrees. However, with the 74% humidity it feels more like 45.

I sit surrounded by the other volunteers.

A twenty-three year old Portuguese volunteer vet – who is dressed in deep red scrubs – called Joana Tavares arrives with her lunch. Joana is here for a month.

We chat. I surprise Joana by talking in Spanish. I am a little *rusty*, but she understands me. She has a large bag of spiky red rambutan fruit that I have seen everywhere, but have yet to try. They are like large, armored grapes – very tasty.

After lunch, Maria heads back to run A4 alone; I have to go to the office to get more photos from the Drop Box program.

The office is humming with activity. There are about ten people at different tables, most lean over laptops, while some are working on desktop computers. It is a mix of Thai's and Europeans.

Everyone is busy.

Paul is there. He shows me the program again, then points to Ray in the corner, (again) saying if I have any problems Ray will help me out. Gill arrives, and Paul leaves with her. A few days later, I receive a link via email – Ray has created a Drop Box and put all the photos in I requested.

I sit going through hundreds of photos of the dog hospitals build. Clicking through one after another.

After an hour, and a long list of photos, I head back to the guest hut. Paul is there. He was supposed to be meeting the electrician who had arranged a meeting. The man was two hours late. "Thai time," Paul says.

There is a friendly couple from Ireland, who are there for a few hours to walk the dogs.

John Dalley is walking around, giving a VIP tour to three people.

I head over to the cat runs to finish my day with some feline therapy.

At 4:00, I head back to the guest hut to take notes before everything vanishes from my inert brain.

At 4:30, the other volunteers start to file back a few at a time. Before long, everyone is sat around chatting, waiting for the truck to take us back to our hotels. They make plans to meet for dinner.

That evening I am lucky enough to eat dinner with five lovely ladies: Maria, Hanna, Lexx, Sina, and Helen. We eat in Pensiri's restaurant down on the sandy beach with the sound of the surf drifting through the darkness. We chat about Soi Dog, and about each other. It is relaxing, informal and enjoyable. Sina and Lexx head back to the hotel, while Maria, Helen, Hannah, and myself pop into Hi Beach, a bar on the beach front for cocktails and beer.

DAY THREE VOLUNTEERING

I still love looking out of the truck at the passing Thai landscape – it never gets old.

It is Brad and Sabina's last day. Tonight they fly home to Australia. They wish they could stay longer. Sabina states that the ten-day experience has put life into a whole new perspective. Things that seemed important before, just aren't. She said it had really opened her eyes. They talk about returning. I believe they will be back – they are so passionate.

I sit down with the other volunteers. I notice a sign on the table; it reads:

1500 survivors

Each in search of 1 hero

Visit bit.ly/Adopt1500

It is a reference to the barbaric dog meat trade. It is a campaign to spread the word, and try to find homes for the 1500 dogs that have been rescued and now live in a Soi Dog-funded purpose built shelter in Buriram.

Maria leads the way to run A4.

When we arrive, all sixteen of *our* dogs are gone, and there are two new ones in their place?

Huh?

It turns out *our* dogs have been moved to the overflow run at the end.

The normal run has a little mud but is mainly cleanable concrete – easy to hose down. The new run is mostly mud, which becomes apparent the instant we enter, and within a minute, we are covered in mud from the excited, jumping dogs. Plus, the gate is very wide, so as we walk in, Lindsey slides right past. As we get her back in, Dr. Who escapes. As we get him back, Lindsey makes another dash for it – they are like wet eels in a bucket.

© Dr. Who saying good morning.

We eventually walk Na Tong and Apple, followed by a list of the others in their pecking order.

The three-legged black dog called Trin decides she wants to get into the lake. The dogs are not allowed off the lead, (unless it's in their run or the enrichment area), but if you give them enough slack, and time, they will dart into the water. Trin was more of a slow ambling slide down into the lake to cool off from the sweltering Thai heat.

© Wawa, slowly walking around the lake on three legs.

There is a new little dog in the run today called Wawa. She only has three legs and was absent the day before due to treatment.

Wawa is calm and gentle, and I instantly have a new favorite in run A4 (sorry Dr. Who). She recently had a leg amputated due to being hit by a car. As I walk her around the lake, she has to take constant rests. She is quiet, obedient and never pulls on the lead.

I take three times longer with her just to do one lap. But I enjoy the pace. Once the physiotherapy and hydrotherapy room is complete in the new dog hospital, it is dogs like Wawa who will reap the benefits.

The time goes too quickly when you enjoy the company of the dogs. Before I know it, it is lunchtime again. However, today we are not getting a delivery; we all jump into the back of a truck and head to a restaurant around the corner. The black plastic on the back of the open-air truck is red hot from sitting in the sun. Everyone does their best to try to sit without touching anything.

As the truck picks up speed, the cool breeze is refreshing. Before long, we are at a small family-run restaurant. There are about ten things on the menu, you point and then sit down and the food is cooked fresh and placed in front of you. We are all on one long table that already has some of the office staff sat eating. Paul, Darren and his wife Deb, and a few others chat among themselves. We join in with the conversation.

Next to the restaurant is the first 7-Eleven I have seen in Phuket. I purchase a pot of chicken and ham mayonnaise, and a cake-type bun with luminous green custard inside, (the custard is so green it looks like it will glow in the dark).

Before long, we are back at Soi Dog. As the others wander back to their runs, I sit to catch up on some notes.

It is much busier today. There is a large family of at least ten people (they are hard to count, they never stay still long enough) from Australia, who have been helping for the day, walking dogs from the OAP and Small Dogs runs.

There is also a young couple helping out for the day, and an older husband and wife, and another family with four children.

Inga, Darren and Diana are really busy answering questions, taking people on tours, and getting merchandise that the people want to buy – tee-shirts, hats, etc.

Another man and woman arrive with a small child who instantly goes over and sits down in a deep puddle of water.

Even though I only spend three days walking the dogs, and interacting with them, I can understand why the volunteers fall in love with the dogs in *their* run. On Facebook, I see posts from people who have volunteered at Soi Dog asking others for photos of their favorite dogs, or asking questions about particular animals they have fallen in love with.

Now I understand how they feel.

Some of the volunteers fall so hard they end up adopting dogs in *their* runs, taking them back to their country once everything has been arranged.

Everything now makes sense, why so many people volunteer – the feeling you receive helping out, interacting so closely with the dogs, really has a deeply profound effect on you.

For me, it makes the whole experience even more rewarding and real. It makes me hope my book does well, creating more revenue to go towards helping these amazing animals.

They were once stray animals that had no real

hope for the future. Now, with Soi Dog's help, possible from donations from people like you, these animals will spend the rest of their lives being loved and protected, and hopefully adopted into caring forever homes.

© Sabina Archibald with Gypsy in Run A1.

I have just heard from Sabina on Facebook; she has booked a return trip to stay three months next year. As I said, volunteering at Soi Dog is addictive – it puts life into perspective.

A HAPPY ENDING – ANIMALS RESCUED

There are some truly heartwarming stories concerning a few of the rescue animals at Soi Dog. We have collected some for you to enjoy.

16

SHIVER'S STORY

An average example of just one abandoned puppy…

Hi, my name is Shiver. When I was just four months old, I lived all alone in an abandoned drain beside a busy main road. I don't remember how I got there, or where I come from, as I was very sick, and I thought I was going to die, due to being too weak to scavenge for food, and only having dirty water to drink.

Luckily for me, one of the thousands of passing drivers found me and took pity on me, and delivered me to the Soi Dog Foundation.

The people at Soi Dog looked after me and made me better, and wanted nothing in return. I was underweight and dehydrated and had no hair, and I was covered in mange, but they showed me love and took care of me – they didn't see a lost cause.

After my treatment, I feel much better and now have many new friends in my Run, and they are doing everything in their power to find me a forever home, where I can live out the rest of my life with a caring family who will love me for who I am.

Soi Dog has many puppies just like me.

© Shiver before and after.

17

CHARMANDER'S STORY

Soi Dog received a frantic call from someone saying they could hear a distressed animal, which sounded like a puppy, and it was stuck down a very deep hole. The person said they could hear the animal but could not see it.

When the rescue team arrived, they realized the hole was too deep to simply climb down. Animal rescue officer Khun Nok had to be slowly lowered down by a rope.

However, the puppy was no longer making a sound by the time the rescuers arrived. They hoped they weren't too late, and would simply be retrieving a limp body.

It wasn't until Khun Nok reached the puppy, he realized it was just hanging onto life. Another hour or so and it would have been all over.

However, Charmander, (he was named after a

Pokémon character that has a flame on its tail, which indicates a life force, because the little puppy was fighting to stay alive) was in a terrible, heartbreaking condition.

© Animal rescue officer Khun Nok being lowered into the deep hole.

Charmander was very weak and dehydrated, and covered in ticks and fleas. His tiny body was also covered in injuries from his fall into the deep pit.

He desperately needed medical help.

The barely conscious puppy was rushed to the Soi Dog clinic where they could start administering treatment immediately.

Charmander was redehydrated and inoculated, and his cuts treated. He then had to undergo a series of medical baths to heal his skin.

The little puppy looked so serious and sad, and for a while never wagged his tail – understandably.

The vets wondered if he would ever show signs of recovery and happiness, or would he take a turn for the worse, having been through such a traumatic event?

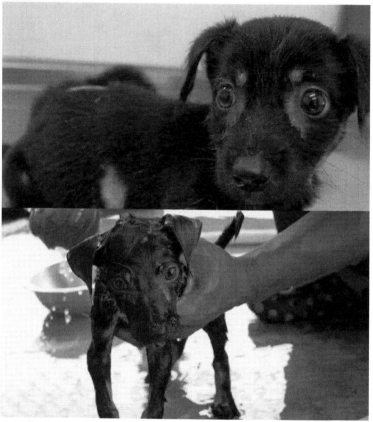

© Charmander after treatment, and during a medical bath.

Luckily, after a week of treatment, he started to perk up enough to be moved to the Puppy Run, where he is now thriving, thanks to people's contributions that allow Soi Dog to help animals in need.

© Charmander, all happy and healthy.

18

MIRACLE, A THAI DOG MEAT TRADE SURVIVOR, WINS PRESTIGIOUS CRUFTS AWARD

The amazing bond between a severely disabled six-year-old boy and his Thai rescue dog was recognized on Sunday 8th March at the Crufts 2015 dog show. Miracle, rescued from Thailand's illegal dog meat trade and adopted by the Leask family in Strathglass, Scotland, beat over two hundred other entrants to pick up the prestigious Crufts Eukaneba Friends for Life award.

Yet just a couple of years ago, things looked much different for the Thai crossbreed. Miracle was snatched from the streets of north east Thailand and loaded onto a truck with hundreds and hundreds of other stolen dogs, all destined for the dog meat restaurants of Hanoi in Vietnam.

Luckily for Miracle, the truck carrying him to

what would have been a slow and agonizingly painful death was intercepted by agents working for the Soi Dog Foundation, who've been fighting the illegal trade for five years. The dogs were taken to a purpose-built shelter in north east Thailand, and adopters were sought.

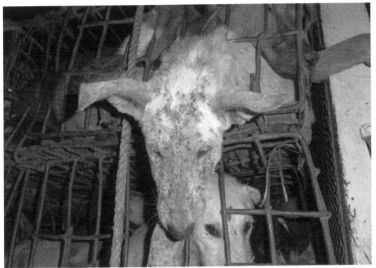

© Miracle, shortly after being rescued in Thailand.

Amanda Leask spotted Miracle's photo shortly after he'd been rescued on a Soi Dog Facebook post. Devastated by his plight and the hopelessness of his situation, she enquired about adopting him. Already an owner of three rescue dogs from Soi Dog, Amanda was about to get her fourth.

Amanda's six-year-old son, Kyle, was born with cerebral palsy, and was later diagnosed with autism. It is incredibly difficult for him to communicate with his family. Amanda decided to adopt some small dogs to be company for him, having heard that

autistic people can develop extremely close relation-
ships with dogs. Miracle is the latest of them, but it's
Kyle and Miracle who have developed a remarkably
close bond, where there appears to be a completely
unspoken mutual understanding.

As Amanda says: "They've both faced so much
hardship in their lives; it's like there's an unspoken
language between them. When Kyle gets upset
because he can't convey what he wants to, Miracle
will go and lay at his side for Kyle to touch and
stroke. Miracle seems to automatically know when
Kyle needs him."

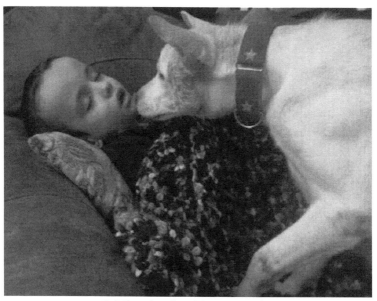

© Miracle checking on Kyle.

Amanda added: "If Kyle simply wants some
attention, Miracle will go over and shower him with
kisses. And it works the other way too. Kids can

build up confidence in dogs where they seek solace, and Miracle gets this in abundance from Kyle."

The unique bond between man and dog is still yet to be explained fully. But Amanda knows how much it has helped Kyle. "He seems so much happier in the presence of Miracle. It's like they're soul mates."

Miracle won £1,500 for his Crufts award, and Amanda shared the money between Soi Dog and the Autistic Society.

© Best friends Miracle and Kyle.

19

MARLEY'S STORY

Another example is Marley; a female aged about two years, who was brought to the shelter in March 2014. Aside from the cigarette burns to her face, she had machete wounds on both back paws. It was suggested that the wounds were deliberately inflicted, as each paw had a clean criss-cross cut which had severely damaged the nerves. It meant that the paws pointed backwards, rather than forwards.

The wounds were cleaned, and the paws were bandaged daily in order to keep them in the correct position whilst the nerves repaired themselves.

It took over two months of steady, patient treatment at the Soi Dog clinic for Marley to start making a recovery, and fortunately, thanks to the efforts of the people in charge of adoptions at Soi Dog; she was adopted by Heather and Mike Jess from

Seattle, USA in July 2014. Marley's adopters were made fully aware of her condition, and knew that she would need a lot of expensive specialist vet treatments in the USA before she could walk again, yet they selflessly welcomed Marley into their family.

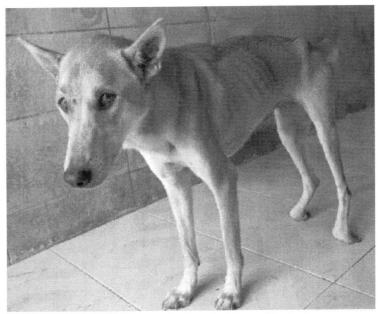

© Marley on arrival at Soi Dog, Phuket.

Thanks to the expert medical care she has been receiving, Marley has now learnt to balance and walk again, but still needs to wear special "boots."

That should be the end of the story. But unfortunately in early August 2014, Marley was diagnosed with a rare form of cancer. Heather and Mike are determined to beat the illness, and Marley is currently undergoing eight rounds of chemo-therapy, costing three hundred and sixty dollars per round. There will also be continued checkups, which starts at one thousand and three hundred dollars. The Jess family have started a fundraising initiative on the GoFundMe website to raise enough money to cover the treatment, and are hoping to raise just over four thousand dollars to cover the cost.

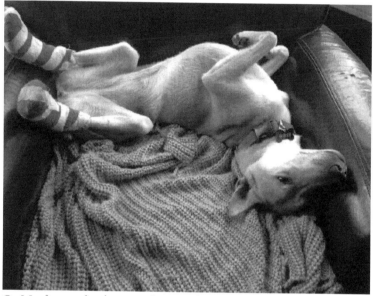

© Marley relaxing at home in Seattle on her favorite couch, with her socks on to protect her sensitive paws.

20

DUMBO GETS ADOPTED BY ESSEX (UK) FAMILY

It's very difficult to understand sometimes just why people abuse or neglect defenseless animals. In March 2014, Soi Dog Foundation, received a distress call from an anxious lady in the south of the island, who was concerned about her neighbor's dog. The lady explained that she could see into her neighbor's front yard, and that for the past few months, a dog had been tied up tightly there by a chain round its neck, attached to a pole. She was worried over the health of the dog, and wanted someone to come down and take a look at it.

The lady explained that there was no shade for the dog to hide from the blazing heat of the sun. She also said that there never seemed to be any water provided for the dog, and that she had never seen the dog being fed. The dog looked, she said, anemic, and would bark constantly as if it was trying to attract attention from passersby. She also said that the animal was most likely in severe pain, as she could hear the yelps and whimpers whenever the dog stopped barking for a minute.

Khun Jaroon, one of the animal rescue officers at Soi Dog, raced down to the house immediately, and was shocked to find Dumbo exactly as the lady had described. He was able to quickly cut away the chain using bolt cutters, just as Dumbo collapsed on the floor, heat exhaustion taking its toll.

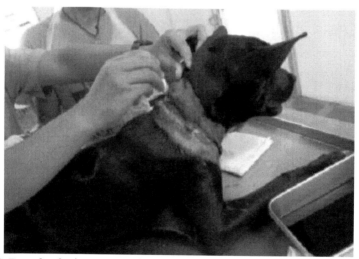

© Dumbo being treated at the Soi Dog Clinic. A deep neck injury from the chain.

Dumbo was brought to Soi Dog's shelter where a team of vets was waiting to treat him. He had a deep laceration around his neck where the chain that had kept him a prisoner for so long had worn away the fur and skin, cutting deep into the flesh. One vet, Dr Sai, cleaned and sterilized the wound, and applied cream and bandages. The other vets set about rehy-

drating Dumbo, and started administering medication to help with the anemia he was suffering.
Dumbo also received food supplements to help
speed up his recovery. He weighed just ten kilos
when he arrived at the shelter, and looked in a
dreadful condition.

© Dumbo in his new home in Essex UK.

After a few weeks of intensive treatment, Dumbo
started making good progress, and was moved to

one of the Soi Dog shelter runs to continue his rehabilitation.

Dumbo would not have been safe if Soi Dog had returned him to his owner once he was completely recovered. Instead, it was decided to put him up for adoption. A lady called Pauline Hall from Essex saw Dumbo on Soi Dog's Facebook post, fell in love with him, and decided to adopt. Dumbo flew from Thailand to his forever home in November 2014, and both have never looked back.

"He is absolutely adorable," says Pauline. "He gets on really well with his sister, a Staffie called Princess Sasha Bean, and he's made our family complete.

I can't imagine life without him. Even though he's a little monkey at times, stealing my shoes, we love him to bits."

Dumbo's favorite foods are chicken and banana, and his second best friend is Bentley, Pauline's older dog. They get on really well, Pauline stated. Dumbo's obviously learnt to bark in English.

21

WHY SOI DOG DOES IT?

WARNING: There are graphic photos in this chapter showing injured animals

The tragic plight of the neglected and homeless animals in Phuket and other provinces throughout Thailand is the sole reason the Soi Dog Foundation was established in 2003. Soi Dog has made a significant and noticeable impact in improving the lives of tens of thousands of animals and continues to expand its support for homeless, abused and neglected animals.

Soi Dog Foundation is the only organization on Phuket which has a help line and responds to emergency calls.

Each month, Soi Dog spends tens of thousands of dollars treating, neutering and spaying sick and injured dogs and cats. Sadly, many of which are the victims of cruelty.

Some people say that saving the life of one animal does not change the world. However, it does change the world for that individual animal, and that is the whole point. Soi saves them one at a time – each one is as important as the next.

© Rawai. Before and after.

Rawai, pictured above, was chained up at a restaurant at Rawai beach, and left to die. The photo to the right shows a month later, when he is on his way to recovery.

© Buddy. Before and after.

© Inas. Before and after.

Many animals are chained up, or locked away, so they can't even scavenge for food. Some that are found resemble skeletons, with mere days of life left in them.

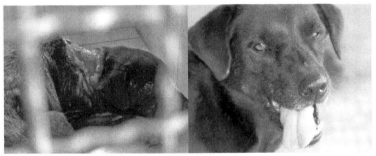

© Dam Dam. Before and after.

Machete attacks are common against street dogs. Left untreated most will die an agonizing death. Dam Dam (above) was one of the lucky ones, when someone reported his condition to Soi Dog.

Animals that can be returned to their original locations are returned when fully recovered.

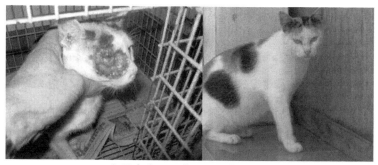

© Trixie. Before and after.

© Humphrey. Before and after.

A SHOCKING CASE OF ANIMAL CRUELTY

Since Thailand introduced its first ever Animal Welfare Law in December 2014, Soi Dog's undercover investigators have been ruthless in pursuing animal abusers through the judicial system to ensure justice is served.

Recently, an officer from the country's Health Department came upon a shocking sight in Kanchanaburi, in western Thailand.

A live dog was found with its lower half-buried in the ground, causing it to be pinned down, unable to move. The officer found the dog at a campground housing immigrant laborers, of whom Thailand has many.

On investigation, it emerged, they were planning to eat the dog as part of a dish known as *Coconut Dog.*

This barbaric practice is when the lower half of the dog's body is buried below the ground – compressed in wet mud – for anything from two weeks to a month. During that time, the dog would be in constant pain, and force-fed coconut milk, along with just enough food to keep it alive.

The twisted belief is that this would cause the dog's fur (which is buried below the mud) to slide off, after which the rest of the dog would be skinned alive and its meat grilled. It was believed that the feeding of coconut milk to the animal would give the meat a more fragrant flavor.

Soi Dog's undercover investigators coordinated with the police to arrest the person responsible, who will now face criminal proceedings under Thailand's new Animal Welfare law.

The dog is now being cared for at a clinic in Kanchanaburi. He is unable to walk and suffering from an infection around his lower body, partly from lying in his own urine. He will need physical therapy in the future in order to get him walking again, once he has completed treatment for his infection.

The great news is that now Dam (meaning "black colour" in Thai) is standing and using all four legs again, and continues to make progress every day.

Once he has fully healed, the volunteers caring for him will seek a forever home for Dam and are already receiving many offers from kind-hearted animal lovers who have been touched by his story.

Soi Dog will not give up fighting animal cruelty and continuing to raise awareness that such practices are now illegal in Thailand, and are completely barbaric and unacceptable.

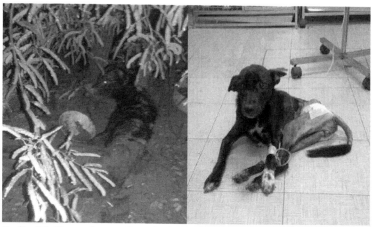

© (Left) Dam just after being rescued. (Right) Back at the clinic.

Animals that have been ill treated or abused, or whose treatment has taken many months and will no longer be accepted in their original habitat remain in the shelter. These animals often make great pets and are available for adoption:

www.soidog.org/en/adoptions/

Those animals which cannot be adopted or returned to their original habitat are available for sponsorship:

www.soidog.org/en/sponsor-a-
dog-or-cat/Default.aspx

Because of Soi Dog's no kill policy, some animals
have been at the facility for almost a decade.

22

SPONSORING A DOG

My name is Soozie Hall from England, and I have been to Thailand many times in the last twenty years and have always been aware of the situation with the stray dog population on Phuket.

A few years ago, when I was visiting, I heard of a man who goes around Phuket looking after the packs of stray dogs giving them food, water, and medical attention whenever he is able.

Every time I returned to Phuket I would ride around on my motorbike until I found him, and help him out, to the best of my ability.

At this time, I was truly unaware of Soi Dog, until I learned about them from one of my favorite authors Facebook page, as I followed Glen Johnson's travels around Asia.

While chatting to Glen through social media I heard about the Soi Dog Foundation. After checking out the amazing work they do I decided to sponsor a dog – online – in their Phuket facility, called Na Tong.

On my next trip to Phuket, I am really looking forward to becoming a volunteer at Soi Dog, and meeting Na Tong in person.

Please help this noble cause, because the way I look at it is, you play the lottery every week, and you may win, but more often than not you don't. How about putting some of that money into a definite win and sponsor a dog? An animal that desperately needs you, or medical supplies. Every penny will help these beautiful animals.

Soozie Hall
(September 2015)

© Na Tong at Soi Dog Phuket. (Run A4 – the same run I volunteered in).

VOLUNTEER'S STORIES

Soi Dog wouldn't be what it is today without the continued support of volunteers from all around the world – people who give up their time to help in any way they can. Here are some of their stories.

23

ALEX'S STORY – HOW I CHANGED MY LIFE

On the surface, you would think Alex Wainwright had everything. Nice house, new car, great friends and family, and an international jet-set lifestyle as a senior cabin crew with British Airways.

"I loved visiting New York the best," says Alex, thirty-six and from West Sussex. "It's such a cosmopolitan city, and it never sleeps. We had some great parties there. Tokyo is a fantastic place to visit as well, although I had real problems with the language."

But after eight grueling years of flying, Alex began to question what she was doing with her life. The time she spent away from her friends and family had begun to take its toll, but more than that, Alex did not feel like she was making any great contribution to society by looking after airline passengers.

"I just began to question everything, like how important was money, did I really want to spend the rest of my life flying around the world, and what did I really want to do in life to make a positive contribution to society? That was the thing that really got me; I did not feel as if I was making a positive difference."

© Alex at Soi Dog's Phuket.

During a rare break on a long-haul flight one day, Alex picked up a copy of the Daily Mail and began to flick through the pages. She came across a headline which read, "This Article Will Change Your Life!" and began to read through. It was about a lady

186

in England, who had adopted a street dog from Thailand, from a dog and cat welfare charity called Soi Dog, based in Phuket. Something clicked in Alex's brain. She had a love of dogs anyway, and was just amazed at what the Soi Dog Foundation was doing to help the street dogs and cats of Thailand. It was the kind of difference that she wanted to make in the world.

A few days later, Alex contacted Soi Dog and asked if she could go and spend a week volunteering at the shelter in Phuket. When the answer came back as yes, Alex booked a flight, and spent a week helping out in March 2014 during one of her holidays. Alex absolutely loved her time at Soi Dog. Her main jobs were dog walking and socializing the animals being kept in the shelter. Many Thai street dogs have had little or no proper interaction with humans, so Alex's role was to spend as much time with them to help them get used to being in the company of humans. This is important, so as the animal can be put up for adoption.

Alex returned to Soi Dog in May 2014, but this time for three weeks, doing the same things. She remembers walking one of the dogs one day at the shelter, and thinking to herself, *how can I quit my job and come here to volunteer full time?*

On her final day at the shelter, Alex was getting psychologically prepared to return to the UK when she was approached by the shelter manager, who asked if she would consider coming back to Soi Dog as a long-term volunteer. She shrieked with joy, and immediately began planning on selling her house and car, quitting her job and returning to Thailand.

Eleven months into her new life, and Alex has no regrets whatsoever. "I love the work here; I get so much satisfaction from helping the sick and injured dogs recover, and from seeing how a dog that does not trust human's changes over time to become happy and content playing with the volunteers. I could not wish for more, and consider myself so lucky. This is what I was meant to do."

24

DEB AND DARREN BENBROOK'S STORY

Deb and Darren Benbrook, both in their early forties, hail from Leeds in West Yorkshire. Deb was a marketing assistant in the food industry, and Darren was a self-employed taxi driver. They lived a very comfortable lifestyle, surrounded by friends and family, so on the surface; everything was fine. But during 2010, family tragedy struck, when they lost several close relatives in succession. The losses really affected both of them, and it struck them how unpredictable life can be. Anything could be around the corner.

At the same time, both Deb and Darren were getting tired of the rat race they found themselves in. As Debs says, "We were fed up of working to live and keeping up with the Jones'. We both wanted to make a fresh start, do something more constructive with our lives, give something back to society and live a simpler life without all the trappings of the western world."

One evening after a tough day at work, Deb and Darren sat around their kitchen table to discuss what they were going to do. It took just five minutes to decide to sell their house, cars and all their possessions, and to set off on a trip around the world to find what they were looking for that had been missing from their lives for so long.

They flew to New York first, and spent some time there before heading to San Francisco and exploring the national parks in California. From there they flew to Santiago in Chile, and got jobs running a hostel in Pucon. "We loved it there," said Deb, "It was really tough work, but we met some really amazing people and loved the local culture." Two months later, they headed south before the winter set in, traveling through Argentina, Bolivia and Peru, before heading back to Chile to run another hostel for six months.

In February 2012, Deb and Darren flew to New Zealand, a country they had always wanted to visit, and worked in the orchards of Motueka for nine months. They loved the simple life there, but were still looking for that real meaning or purpose in life that had been evading them for so long.

From New Zealand, they flew to Singapore in November 2012, and then made their way through Malaysia to Koh Phangan in Thailand, where they worked in a beach resort over the Christmas and New Year period, followed by project management of an apartment complex there. However, it still was not what they were looking for.

Finally, in 2014 Deb and Darren arrived in Phuket, and were told about a dog and cat welfare charity there called Soi Dog, who was looking after the stray population. Deb and Darren had looked after a street dog on Koh Phangan for the time they were there, recognizing the fact that no-one was caring for the strays, so they immediately felt like they had a bond with Soi Dog. They enquired about volunteering at the Soi Dog shelter in the north of the island, and were told they would be very welcome, given the charity relied heavily on volunteers to help the animals. Deb and Darren jumped at the chance.

© Darren and Deb at Soi Dog Phuket.

One year on, Deb is now the volunteer adoptions manager, in charge of finding homes for the three and a half thousand dogs and cats that Soi Dog cares for. Darren is the volunteer coordinator, making sure that jobs are assigned across the twenty or so volunteers who come to the shelter daily.

So is this what they were looking for?

"We love helping out here. It gives us a real purpose in life. Helping the animals, meeting new cats and dogs and seeing them develop into adoptable pets. The drive and dedication of the people here is incredible. Everyone working to the one common goal of improving the welfare of dogs and cats. This is where we want to be," added Deb.

25

MARK AND DIANA VAN DE WALL'S STORY

Mark and Diana van der Wall, both Dutch and now in their mid forties, have a very interesting life story to tell. Diana held a steady job running an after-school club for kids in The Netherlands, before changing to work with the terminally ill. Mark was never really a corporate person, and moved from job to job, trying to find something that interested him. He sold insurance, was a truck driver, a delivery man, a garbage collector, and at one stage, he even bred snakes to make a living. Both, however, were becoming increasingly frustrated by life in The Netherlands; the cost of living, over-population, lack of good job opportunities, and the limitations and frustrations of living a 9 to 5 working life.

They had always dreamed of moving to Surinam, a former Dutch colony in South America, bordered by French Guiana, Guyana and Brazil to the south. So in 2006, they sold their house, car and all their possessions, and flew off to their new life with just a couple of backpacks as a reminder of their past lives.

They spent four months living in an abandoned house deep in the Surinam jungle. Their water came from a well in the garden, and they bought a dirt bike so they could get to the local market twice a week to sell thirty different kinds of fruit that they collected every day from the jungle around their house.

Life was great for a while, but the dangers of the environment were ever-present, so they decided to move to the relative safety of the capital, Paramaribo, and found work in a guest house there.

Diana set up a foot massaging business, and Mark became the guest house handyman. When the owner decided to take a one-year holiday in Europe, Mark and Diane took over the day to day management of the guest house.

"It was great fun, really hard work, but we had a very good time and met many interesting people," said Mark.

After two years in Surinam, they decided to leave, traveling first to French Guiana and then on to Brazil.

"Surinam is a lovely country; we loved our time there, but we knew we could not live there forever," Diana stated. "There were not enough opportunities for us, and we never really found what we were looking for."

Brazil, on the other hand, was booming economically at the time, and presented Mark and Diana with many new opportunities. However, the van der Walls did not like Brazil, and decided that they needed to once and for all choose what kind of life they wanted. After several discussions, they agreed that they wanted to do charity or non-government organization work, preferably with children.

They set off back to Europe to earn some money, with the intention of leaving The Netherlands as soon as they had enough funds to last for a few years. Diana set up a business doing foot massage, and Mark worked as a garbage collector. It was still 9 to 5 work, but at least they knew there would be an end to it after twelve months.

When Mark and Diana had enough money to travel again, they flew, firstly, to Thailand, then on to Malaysia, where they found work in a children's nursery. But unfortunately, this became another 9 to 5 scenario that they had so desperately wanted to avoid, so they went back to Thailand and found work in an orphanage in Sangkhlaburi, on the border with Burma.

The orphanage housed a hundred and fifty children, and the van der Wall's loved working there. Diana helped out with the children, whilst Mark took care of all the animals. Mark also helped out from time to time at a small dog shelter next door to the orphanage, and this is where his passion for dogs started.

"I had never owned a dog before, so I had no idea how loving and trusting these animals are," Mark stated. "However much love and attention you give them, they give it back ten-fold. They are truly amazing creatures."

Mark learned from the small dog shelter that they were being partially funded at the time by a Thai-based dog and cat welfare charity called Soi Dog. Soi in Thai means "street." This was to become an important part of the future for Mark and Diana.

After four years, the van der Wall's decided that it was time to move on again. They wanted to be closer to the sea, and Mark's growing love of dogs was pushing him in the direction of working for some kind of dog rescue charity. Diana had been brought up surrounded by dogs, and was also keen to follow Mark's idea. So in the summer of 2012, Mark contacted John Dalley, co-founder and vice president of Soi Dog, to see if he needed any volunteers at the shelter in Phuket, Thailand.

The answer was a resounding yes.

Mark was amazed when he arrived at the Soi Dog shelter on his first day of volunteering. Compared with the small shelter in Sangkhlaburi that he had helped out with, it was clean, well organized, well managed, had the right facilities to treat and shelter the animals, and was run by compassionate people who only wanted the best for the animals.

As another volunteer coordinator, Mark loves the chance he gets everyday to meet new people from around the world who either help out at, or who are just visiting, the Soi Dog shelter. And he just loves the time he gets to spend with the dogs.

"I love the work here; it's just so rewarding to be able to make a positive difference to the lives of these street dogs."

Diana is the same. "We've found our heaven on

earth. We love what we do here."

© Mark and Diana at Soi Dog Phuket.

26

SPENCER'S STORY

Spencer Hardy, thirty-four, was a London-based computer software engineer doing the grinding daily commute into north west London from south London everyday. The bus, train, tube and walk journey took ninety minutes each way, and was beginning to take its toll. With no option to buy or rent an apartment closer to work, due to the high cost of housing in central London, Spencer could not see a solution for the situation he was in.

"I really enjoyed my job, but I hated my lifestyle so much," he said. Working eleven hours a day, with three hours commuting time, meant that by the time Spencer got home each evening, all he wanted to do was to go to bed. His social life was suffering, and he knew, deep down, that this was not the life he wanted to lead.

One weekend, when Spencer was working at his

computer at home, a new email arrived. It was from a friend of his who had quit his job to travel around the world. The friend was then in Australia, and sent Spencer some pictures of the Great Barrier Reef, together with a quick summary of the other places he'd visited, and the people he met during his travels.

Something immediately clicked with Spencer. He did not really know what he wanted to do with his life, but he knew he was not going to find the answer in London. So first thing on Monday morning, Spencer handed in his notice at work, and began planning a twelve-month holiday trip across Asia and Australasia. He felt as if a huge weight had been lifted from his shoulders.

Spencer's first stop in Asia was at the paradise island of Phuket, in Thailand. He rented a house and scooter, and actively began to integrate into the local community, something he had never had the time to do in London.

On his street, there were four stray dogs, which used to scavenge through the rubbish bins for food. Very wary of humans, the dogs kept their distance from Spencer at first. However, Spencer, taking pity on them, decided to take responsibility for feeding them everyday. Slowly, over time, the dogs came to trust him. When he was away, they would wait outside his house for him to come home, and greet him with yelps of delight and wagging tails.

One day, Spencer noticed a tumor on one of the dogs. He could not take the dog to the vet because he only had a scooter, so instead he took some pictures of the tumor and took them to a local vet to ask what he could do. The vet gave him some medication to give to the dog, but it had little or no effect. A couple of weeks later, the dog started to become quite aggressive, and Spencer knew he must be in pain. Then he remembered a Thai friend of his who had told Spencer of a dog and cat welfare charity in Phuket called Soi Dog. They had a shelter in Mai Khao in the north of the island, and the shelter had some vets and a clinic that would treat street dogs and cats free of charge.

Spencer jumped on his scooter and set off on the long journey up to Soi Dog to see if they could help. He was met at the shelter by Diana, one of the long-term volunteers at Soi Dog. She took him to the shelter office where a Thai lady called May listened to his story. May told Spencer that they would send a truck down to his house later that day to pick up the dog and bring it back to the shelter for assessment and treatment. By the time Spencer got back home, the Soi Dog truck was waiting for him. They found the dog, Buster, a six-year-old female, and she was taken up to the Soi Dog shelter.

Buster had TVT, a form of cancer. The Soi Dog vets removed the tumor, and Buster was given five weeks intensive treatment to ensure she became completely cancer-free. Once Buster had recovered and gone through a period of recuperation, the Soi Dog truck brought Buster back to Spencer's house, where she now lives.

Spencer was so overwhelmed by the compassion shown by Soi Dog to Buster that he wanted to pay them back. He offered his services as a volunteer at the shelter, and ten months later he's still there. He's now the Adoptions Logistics coordinator, making sure that the dogs being adopted get to their new homes safely.

So has Spencer found his true vocation in life by mistake?

"When I wake up in the morning now, I can't wait to jump on the scooter and get to the shelter. The love the dogs show you is just amazing. Being able to help them have better lives is so rewarding; I never had this feeling in London. I know I'm making a real difference to hundreds and thousands of dogs who otherwise would be living lives of misery."

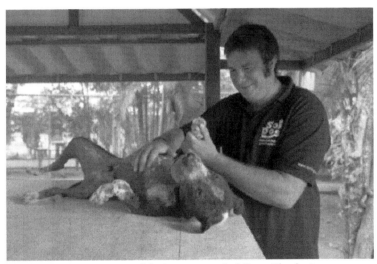

© Spencer with Benny at Soi Dog Phuket.

27

MARTIN TURNER'S STORY

Martin Turner is forty-six and graduated with a degree in International Marketing.

He started out his career working in advertising in London, for a global advertising agency called McCann-Erickson, as a strategic planner, then moved on to global account management. His client list was impressive, with giants like Nestle. His business encompassed around $500 million, and he was running campaigns for them in a 115 different countries.

A big part of his job was meetings at Nestle HQ in Switzerland, to present campaigns, and discuss strategies.

Martin enjoyed his job, and when they asked him to join the company at the Switzerland HQ, to help run the global marketing and advertising section, he jumped at the chance.

He was ready for a change. It was time to leave London behind.

Martin spent six years trying to improve their media and marketing functions, and was relatively successful.

As it turned out, he wasn't enjoying working at Nestle HQ, there were just too much politics and bureaucracy that were holding him back.

So, Martin asked if he could go and be a Communication Director in another country.

They didn't want to lose him, so they agreed to his request.

He was moved to central and west Africa, based in Ghana. His job was to centralize the marketing and advertising in twenty-six African countries.

It was a tough job, but Martin enjoyed the challenge, and he loved Africa. However, as all good things do, after three years, it came to an end when his contract expired.

Martin had two options, go back to the Switzerland HQ, or leave the company and do something else.

Martin couldn't stomach the idea of going back to the petty politics and bureaucracy, so he decided to leave and set up his own marketing consultancy company – he had the knowledge and the background to set out on his own.

As his company grew, he started to do jobs all around the world, and even though he enjoyed what he was doing, he had a nagging feeling that whilst all was well and good, earning a good living doing something he enjoyed, he felt like he wasn't making a difference and contributing to the world in a positive way. There're already too many selfish people in the world, and he didn't want to become someone who is only interested in money.

Martin decided he wanted to do something that actually benefited someone or something else, other than just worrying about himself.

He started researching the not-for-profit sector. At first, there was so much to choose from – so many worthy charities – the environment, orphaned children, and animals.

He was overwhelmed.

© Martin at Soi Dog Phuket.

Then, one day, Martin phoned John Dalley, who he knew socially from his trips to Phuket to visit his brother-in-law.

Martin was aware that John had set up Soi Dog with his wife Gill, so he tapped into John's knowledge about opportunities in Thailand – he had always wanted to spend more time in South-East

Asia.

John put Martin in touch with Leonard (Soi Dog Fundraising Director) and Gregg (Soi Dog CEO at that time). He was told they might have a role for him.

Martin was interested.

Three months after his initial discussion with John, Martin was at the shelter in Phuket with his own desk in the office. Martin has been with Soi Dog for just over one year.

"I have never looked back, " Martin says. "I have never been happier, knowing I am making a real difference to real lives."

28

PAUL AND JAN'S STORY

Paul Lloyd and long-term partner Janet Evans have been together since 1996, and as Paul states, "We somehow never bothered to tie the knot."

They first visited Soi Dog over four years ago for a couple of weeks as volunteers. However, Paul didn't get to do much that visit as he contracted dengue fever and ended up spending most of his time in the local Thalang Hospital.

Jan though, thoroughly enjoyed her time with the dogs, and they returned the following year for six weeks.

This increased to three months the year after. On this trip, when Gill realised Paul had a construction background she leaned on him for advice, which morphed into Gill asking, "Could you get back by the end of the summer to oversee the new dog hospital project?"

As a result, Paul has been at Soi Dog Phuket with Jan since early October 2014 as a long term volunteer with the dubious title of Project Manager.

Paul was the managing director for over twenty years of his own building company back in West Wales. The business started small and grew bigger and bigger.

However, the turning point was in the year 2004 when his building company was subjected to a tax investigation that lasted most of the year, which created an incredible amount of stress. What was the outcome? After all the stress and aggravation the government put his company and his private life through, they found his books were out by only £240.

This was also compounded by a bout of ill health.

It all came to a head in December 2004, just after everything in their lives was settling down after the tax inspection, and they took a holiday to Thailand to relax; they were both caught in the devastating Indian Ocean tsunami on Boxing Day.

Paul and Jan were on Phi Phi Island, which was badly hit. 8,150 people were reported to have died in Thailand during the Tsunami, and an estimated 4,000 were in and around Phi Phi Island. 70% of the buildings throughout the island were destroyed. 850 bodies were recovered, with an estimated 1,200 people still missing. 104 children lost one or both parents.

Paul and Jan were lucky to have survived, and they literally had to run for their lives.

The things they witnessed were worse than a nightmare – things they could never scrub from their minds.

They felt helpless being in a foreign country with no possessions (everything was destroyed or washed away). They had no money, no credit or bank cards, no passports, and no clothes apart from what they were wearing.

Eventually, with help, they made it home back to the UK.

The horrors they went through unfortunately meant Jan was suffering post-traumatic stress, which took weeks of counseling to overcome.

Bravely, in April 2005, Jan returned alone to Phi Phi to face the demons she witnessed – to try to get closure and to make sense of it all.

After Jan returned to the UK, they sat down and decided money was not important – they almost lost their lives. Things were slammed into perspective, as only a near-death experience can achieve.

Their dream was to travel and see the world – or at least a fair portion of it.

A life-changing decision was made.

They sold their business, and turned their house into a rental property to create an income, and purchased a small touring caravan for a place of refuge for when they return to the UK.

Since the end of 2005, they have been travelled extensively, returning home during the summer months (nice weather to live in a caravan) and picked up various work before returning to their travels, normally in about October of each year.

However, this year, because of the hospital build it has been the exception; they have spent longer in Thailand, with Paul overseeing the new dog hospital.

They did get to return to the UK though, because they were lucky enough to do a super six trip, which entail taking six dogs to the U.K. via Amsterdam for adopters.

As I write this Jan is actually on the KLM flight with Alex (from Soi Dog) on another super six trip – Jan's third this year.

Gill asked Paul if he could stay while the construction work is at such a crucial stage.

However, Paul will be joining Jan, doing another super six trip in November of 2015, where they will get to go home to Wales for a break.

© Paul and Jan at Soi Dog Phuket, August 2015.

29

JESSIE CRAWLEY'S STORY

I think it takes time until you find a cause that you are truly passionate about. Since first hearing of the Soi Dog Foundation, their stories struck a cord with me, and I have been determined to experience what they do first hand, fund raise, volunteer and spreading awareness.

The Soi Dog Foundation is a non-profit, legally registered charitable organization that makes an amazing difference to the lives of dogs (and cats) in Asia, who sadly suffer from abuse, neglect, homelessness and are victims of the cruel dog meat trade.

In February, I traveled to Thailand for a holiday, less than a week after arriving home, I had booked my next flight. It is an exceptionally beautiful country, but I am eager to explore the devastating hidden secrets involving the animals, often out of sight to tourists.

My trip to the dog shelter in Phuket has been funded for by myself. For the last couple of months, I have put a hold on my excessive spending by cutting out on nights out, buying clothes, having a gym membership and eating out. I have saved my pay checks religiously and managed to raise money to help with my food budget by selling clothes on eBay. Being strict has paid off, my flights and accommodation are now booked and paid in full.

I've had an unexpected response and received touching comments from stranger's thanks to the powers of social media while sharing about my eBay link. Many people seemed keen to donate towards this cause, some mentioning that they are interested in how their money would make a difference. I would like the opportunity to raise awareness while over at the shelter, and fund raise while sharing my experience.

I have a blog about the shelter, the organization, the animals, the people and the work they carry out. Hopefully, this will reach out to the kindness of strangers as well as people who know me and understand how much it means to have the opportunity to travel over.

Volunteering here has been so eye opening in many ways. I have learnt so much more about the organization by experiencing it first hand. This will help me to further spread the word, and I was amazed at how much good they really do with additional projects, such as educating local people and the temple work on top of fighting the dog meat trade and helping abused street animals. By meeting people with similar interests, I have been able to start planning more traveling for next year. I met a girl called Kris, who works closely with animal welfare projects worldwide. She has given me amazing information about these organizations so that I can look into them all and maybe work my traveling around visiting some next year.

Thailand is a beautiful place, but I hope more people who visit would realize that animal abuse is most definitely present.

JESSIE CRAWLEY
(May 2015)

© Jessie Crawley at the Soi Dog shelter, with Heineken. May 2015.

Jessie's Blog:
www.jessiecrawley.blogspot.com/

30

ANDY GIBSON - A VOLUNTEER VET

In January 2013, I spent two weeks doing voluntary veterinary work for the Soi Dog Foundation in Thailand. It is incredible what the foundation has achieved to improve the welfare of stray dogs in Phuket over the last decade under the drive of Gill and John Dalley. The shelter provides treatment and preventative care for the street dogs of Phuket and is also home to around four hundred permanent canine residents.

Our daily workload involved the care and treatment of the endless flow of sick and injured dogs and cats brought in from the streets. During my short visit, I experienced the heartache of a distemper outbreak and the difficulty in treating dogs with severe anemia due to blood parasites, which are endemic to the island. Severe skin disease, wounds and fractures were also common, but the

Soi Dog Foundation gives these very sick animals a chance to live, and it was incredibly rewarding to see them respond to treatment and thrive.

Another major activity at the shelter and mobile neutering clinics around the island was the sterilization and vaccination of dogs so that in the future Phuket will have a smaller, healthier and happier dog population with fewer unowned animals. My surgical skills benefited from operating alongside the senior vet, who operates with the speed and competence that is essential to have an impact on reducing the number of dogs breeding on the island.

I was also impressed by the fantastic work ethic of the Burmese kennel staff who keeps the dogs at the shelter clean and well-fed and who I often found sitting in kennels giving dogs the TLC they ceaselessly crave.

The charity also has ambitious plans to broaden their impact on animal welfare in Thailand in the future; attacking the appalling conditions resulting from the dog meat trade and to build a new hospital which will help to treat dogs from all over Thailand.

My lasting memory from Phuket will always be the incredible nature of the street dogs, who often arrived in terrible conditions, but willingly accepted our treatment, often with a wagging tail. I'd like to extend a huge thank you to all the staff at Soi Dog Foundation for their kindness and hospitality, and I look forward to supporting the charity into the future.

© Voluntary vet Andy Gibson, Jan 2013.

31

HELEN LAWRIE – A VOLUNTEER VET

I recently spent two weeks as a veterinary volunteer at Soi Dog and was immediately struck by the size of the foundation, and the scale of the work involved. It was very different from the other small shelters I had spent time at in the past. It became very obvious from the outset what a dedicated; caring and hard-working team are present, and I felt very welcome and proud to be part of it for a short time.

My day to day role involved treating the dogs in the clinic– ensuring they were healthy enough to be released, sterilizing the street dogs and tending to any of the resident dogs requiring treatment. This could be anything from routine preventative treat-ment– of which a very impressive protocol was in place– to tending wounds, blood sampling, sup-portive treatment and organizing radiographs to be taken at a neighboring practice if required. It was very different and challenging from working in a clinic at home as I witnessed many diseases and conditions that I would never normally encounter, such as a range of blood borne parasites and distemper virus. Although sometimes we were limited in our diagnostics, I was impressed by the quality and quantity of the equipment available– all achievable through charitable donation.

It was so rewarding to learn about the adoption system, and I was not at all surprised many people fell in love with the dogs– they were such lovely natured animals, and I could have taken many home myself.

I would be very keen to return to Soi Dog and hopefully see the new hospital when it is built. It will be such a great benefit to the charity and allow them to carry on such amazing work, on a larger scale.

The hard work and care that was given to the dogs was overwhelming, and I was very grateful to have had the chance to help in a small way.

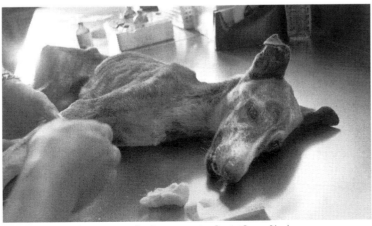

© A stray being treated at the clinic.

32

VOLUNTEERING AND VOLUNTEER'S TESTIMONIALS

The primary role of a volunteer at Soi Dog animal shelter in Phuket, Thailand is to socialize and walk the dogs and socialize the cats and puppies. For dogs and cats at the shelter to be adopted into homes, it is essential to teach them to trust people and to teach the dogs to walk on a lead. Almost all the dogs and cats are former street animals that have never been indoors and they need to learn to feel comfortable around people.

Socialization is especially important for shy animals and those who have been abused.

Many adopters say their new companions are very friendly and comfortable with them, even as soon as they arrive from Thailand – this is because of shelter volunteers.

They particularly need volunteers who enjoy giving tours of the shelter and talking with visitors.

Note: Soi Dog's shelter is open to volunteers from Monday to Friday, 9 am to 5 pm, with a lunch break from 12 to 1.

Soi Dog is open to visitors from 9 am until 3:30 pm.

On your first day, please plan to arrive in time for a tour. Tours are at 9:30 am, 11 am, and 1:30 pm.

Please contact volunteering@soidog-foundation.org for more information about volunteering at the shelter, and email Soi Dog again a couple of days before you come to tell them what day and time you will arrive.

Note: If you simply want to visit and take a tour, you do not need to email Soi Dog, simply turn up at the tour times, and they will be more than happy to show you around.

Here are some testimonials from people who have volunteered their time at the Soi Dog Foundation in Phuket. People who arrived to walk the dogs, or simply sit with the animals to get them used to being around people again – to make them more adoptable.

There are numerous activities at the complex, depending on how you wish to spend your time, and how much energy you have, and how long you can volunteer.

Whatever you choose to do; you will be welcomed with open arms.

"I am so grateful for this experience, and so incredibly impressed with Soi Dog. Thank you for all the work you do for those who have no voice."

Nicole Knapp – New Zealand

"We've had another fantastic time. You have left paw prints on our hearts!"

Paul & Janet – UK

"A huge thank you to Inga for introducing us to Smoocher, and the rest of the brilliant team of people. Smoocher is going to his Forever Home in Hampshire, England with us."

Michelle & Gary – England

"I have had the best three weeks here at Soi Dog. This has been the most rewarding experience ever. Thank you so, so, so much."

Sarah – Scotland

"All the best to all of the two, three, and four-legged ones at Soi."

Suwan & Alex – America

"All the dogs are brilliant, and so are the people working here, and they are so committed to the dogs and cats. I can't wait to return."

Antonia – Switzerland

"The world needs more people like the ones who work and volunteer at the Soi Dog Foundation. We'll be back."

Jenny & Lona – Scotland

"Planned to stay for one week, but we loved it so much here, extended to two weeks. The people at Soi are amazing and worth their weight in gold."

Clare & Kirk – England

"My stay and experience was beautiful. Thank you for everything."

Nerida – Australia

"From the moment we arrived, we both knew we had come to the right place in our hearts."

Robyn & Debbie – Canada

"Fell in love with all the dogs. Can't wait to hear they have all found homes."

Robert – Indonesia

"It's just been an unforgettable time. We didn't plan on adopting any. Jacline and Truffles, we're so excited that you're coming home to Norway with us."

Henning & Mari – Norway

"What a wonderful experience, I will definitely be back. Don't forget to walk the oldies – if you can – they love it."

Maurita - Australia

I had the chance to meet Maurita. She was volunteering at Soi while I was writing the book. Like everyone else there, I was amazed at her zeal and love for the animals.

"It has been delightful working with the dogs and cats, and painting the walls of the A Run."

Keith, Gem, Sophia, and Jeremy - Singapore

"Our past two weeks at Soi Dog have been the best part of our five-month trip in Thailand. We are very excited to bring Jacob (Yindi) back to the US, and for him to be part of our family."

Rose & Samir - USA

"Soi Dog rocks! What a fantastic experience!"

Jackie - Hawaii

"Thank you Soi Dog. Koh Phun Mak Ka."

Ayaka - Japan

"Rewarding is an understatement!"

Rachel & Chris - Wales (UK)

33

SOI DOG PHUKET SHELTER QUESTIONS

How many people work at and for Soi Dog?

Soi Dog have about sixty volunteers and staff, including twenty resident Burmese shelter staff, Thai vets and vet's assistants, Thai mobile sterilization unit staff, Thai animal welfare officers, Thai agents in the north of the country who work on issues related to the dog meat trade, and a group of volunteers who walk and socialize the dogs, and give shelter tours to visitors.

They also have volunteer fundraisers, and volunteers who work in the adoptions team. Soi Dog has very low administration costs; over ninety-one percent of all donations go directly to the animal welfare programmes they run. The remainder goes on local staff wages, operational costs – electricity, fuel for the trucks, etc. – and fundraising.

How many animals are there at the shelter in Phuket at any one time?

Soi Dog has approximately four hundred dogs and forty cats at the shelter at any one time. This obviously varies from week to week. They have two large cat runs attached to the cat clinic, where the cats can be indoors or outdoors depending on how they feel. For the dogs, they have eight mainstream runs and seven specialty runs, each housing between ten and twenty-five dogs. They also have a number of isolation kennels, and a number of recuperation kennels.

Does Soi Dog allow visitors to the shelter in Phuket?

Yes, they welcome visitors to the shelter from 9 am to 12 pm, and again from 1 pm to 3:30 pm, Monday to Friday, all year. During the dry-season – from the end of November to the end of April – please make sure you bring a hat and sun cream.

Guided tours of the shelter are at 9:30 am, 11 am, and 1:30 pm, where a member of the staff will take you on a tour of the whole facility – explaining everything as they move from one section to another, and answering all your questions.

After the tour, you will be welcome to stay on and socialize or play with the dogs and cats.

There is no entrance fee, and all guided tours are also free.

Cold drinking water is freely available (to top up your bottle), and other cold refreshments can be purchased onsite.

Please note the shelter is not open to the public at weekends – the volunteer tour guides have Saturday and Sunday off.

Soi Dog is also on Trip Advisor so you can read reviews from previous visitors prior to coming. At the time of publishing, Soi Dog is classed as the number one "attraction" out of the one hundred and eighty-seven registered on Phuket Island on Trip Advisor. Also, out of the 181 reviews, 179 are five stars, and 2 are four stars – nothing lower.

One of the five-star reviewers on Trip Advisor stated:

"This place is a must-see for any animal lover. We had a great tour with Darren – one of the wonderful volunteers here. The compassion and care shown by this organization is amazing. We took the 1:30 pm tour. Allow a couple of hours (especially if you want a bit of play time with the pups). Although some of the stories are heartbreaking, the overall vibe is just so positive– this organization is making a huge difference and having a positive influence on the conditions for dogs and cats in Thailand. And the work being done in relation to the dog meat trade is invaluable.

"I would highly recommend this tour for families – take your children here, and they will learn so much about compassion and respect for animals. (The Soi tour is

free)."

Helsiewelsie
(2 May 2015)

Another visitor wrote (a five-star review):

"I was so nervous about visiting this refuge as I thought it may be too sad, and I would get too distressed. Luckily, it was simply magnificent.

"When we were in Phuket one year ago I was concerned about two dogs on the beach at our resort (which was one hour from Soi Dog); they were full of ticks, and one had a bad eye. When I returned to Australia, I emailed Soi Dog, and they collected the two dogs the very next day, they sterilized them and treated them and then returned them to their territory. They even sent me pictures of the two dogs while they were at the refuge, so I could relax. I made an on-line donation and vowed to visit Soi Dog on my next trip.

"The place was so clean and tidy and there wasn't even much barking! They are doing a great job here. Volunteers from all over the world help out which is great to see. It is a bit off the beaten track, but if you follow the directions on their website, you will find it. They also list on their website the supplies that they require. So don't turn up empty handed – bring some goodies with you. You can purchase merchandise while you are there or make a donation.

"It is very well run, and the staff are truly caring people. It is extremely hot so take water and wear a hat. Make sure of the tour times as it is really worth it to take

the tour of the facilities. I absolutely loved my visit, and I have great admiration for everyone who helps out there."

Donna1963
(19 April 2015)

Another wrote (a five-star review):

"What a great place! We spent a couple of hours here, but could have stayed all day. If you love dogs and cats, you will love Soi Dog. The rescued animals, some from appalling situations, are well cared for. Food, treatment and care is provided. Free to visit and you can volunteer to walk the dogs if you have the time. Soi Dog is run by donations only, and they have about 400 dogs in their care. A must for the animal lover."

Gina28_11
(August 2015)

Another wrote (a five-star review):

"I volunteered at Soi Dogs for three weeks, and I will be back again next year. It's an amazing place run by very special dedicated people and with a fantastic group of volunteers, many back for return visits. I spent my days walking and helping to socialize the dogs in Run B2, and I didn't want to leave. It was so rewarding, especially when really shy dogs start to trust you and come running for a walk. It's a great place to visit for a short time or even *better to volunteer at for days or weeks."*

Gillian H

(July 2015)

How many animals a year do you treat at the Phuket shelter?

On average, Soi Dog treats around one and a half thousand sick and injured dogs and cats every year at the shelter. However, once the new dog hospital is functional, and the Bangkok sterilization and vaccination programme starts in earnest, we expect this to increase slightly to around one thousand eight hundred animals per year.

How many sterilization operations does Soi Dog carry out every year?

By 2014, Soi Dog was conducting more than seventeen thousand sterilization operations a year, largely in Phuket, but also some in Bangkok.

With the allocation of significant resources to undertake the mass sterilization and vaccination programme in Bangkok, starting in 2015, the target is to carry out up to eighty thousand operations per year from 2016 onwards.

How much does it cost Soi Dog to sterilize one dog or cat?

It costs Soi Dog approximately $20 to sterilize and vaccinate each animal.

Does Soi Dog euthanize street dogs and cats?

Soi Dog will never euthanize any healthy street dog or cat. Our focus is on sterilization, vaccination, treatment, shelter and adoption. In situations where an animal is critically ill, in significant pain and has no chance of making a recovery, Soi Dog will put the animal out of its misery. Every effort will have been made first; however, to bring the animal back to health.

Why is Soi Dog building a new dog hospital at the Phuket shelter, what facilities will it have, and how much will it cost?

The current Soi Dog clinic in Phuket is now far too small to cope for the number of dogs they treat every year, and for the number of vets and vets assistants they have looking after them. The equipment they use is outdated, albeit functional, and they now need more specialist equipment in order for them to be able to treat all the different kinds of diseases and injuries they see everyday.

At present, they do not have the space to put

new equipment in. The kennels in the clinic, which shelter dogs with the most severe problems, are cramped and difficult to disinfect. Most importantly, the clinic lacks appropriate disease control for the number of dogs being treated. They do not have suitable facilities to house the many dogs they treat for contagious illnesses to ensure they cannot infect other animals, and inadequate ventilation lets airborne germs linger. Infectious diseases such as distemper and parvovirus, which are common in Thailand and often deadly, can spread from dog to dog quickly, leading to outbreaks and epidemics.

The facilities at the new hospital will include a fully equipped operating theatre, a physiotherapy room, a radiography room, a treatment room, a dental room, a laboratory, a bathing room, two examination rooms, a supply room, a food pre-paration room, an intensive care unit with eight kennels, an isolation unit with two rooms and twenty kennels, a mother and puppy unit with eleven kennels, and forty-two main kennels, and a veterinary office.

The cost of the new dog hospital for construction and equipment is just over one and a half million dollars.

Is Soi Dog Phuket a 24 hour a day rescue centre for street dogs and cats?

No. Soi Dog office hours are from 8 am to 5 pm on weekdays, and 8 am to 12 pm on the weekends.

However, the telephone hotline is open seven days a week from 8 am to 5 pm. An emergency telephone number is always open outside office hours for life-or-death situations.

Soi Dog would like to be able to rescue dogs and cats twenty-four hours a day, seven days a week, but lacks the funding to be able to do this.

What awards has Soi Dog won since it began operations?

Soi Dog has won several awards over the years.

Co-founder Gill Dalley has been nominated for:

- Asian of the Year (Channel News Asia, Singapore, 2008). The first non-Asian to ever win the award.

- Asia Pacific Canine Hero (2011).

Soi Dog have won:

- The Jeanne Marchig Animal Welfare Award (2011).

- Best Overseas Charity (Wetnose Awards, 2012).

- The Elisabeth Lewyt award from North Shore Animal League (2005).

- It has been honored by Humane Society International (2005) for its achievements.

- And also by the Asia for Animals Conference (2005).

- It's most-recent recognition was the Thai Green Excellence Award for animal welfare (2014).

34

SOI DOG – THE MOVIE WITH JOHN DALLEY

The Soi Dog Foundation released a full-length movie in 2009, and although now out of date, it does give a great insight into the early years of Soi Dog.

Produced by Environment Films and featuring John Dalley.

The full 108-minute movie:

www.soidog.org/en/soi-dogs-the-movie/

35

HOW CAN YOU HELP US HELP THEM?

Soi Dog relies entirely on your donations to continue their much needed work, and as you can see from the book, they are in need of continued support from caring individuals such as yourself.

Your financial support will make an immediate impact in helping the stray and neglected animals.

Help us save a life today.

We encourage you to spread the word about Soi Dog. Even if it's simply liking their Facebook page and sharing their threads and posts, to make them reach the most people possible.

www.facebook.com/SoiDogPageInEnglish

How about signing up for their updates and monthly newsletter to keep you up-to-date with everything they are doing?

www.soidog.org/en/newsletter-sign-up/

Or are you able to organize an event to raise money?

Of course, the most effective way you can make a difference in the lives of these animals is by sponsoring a dog or cat today.

www.soidog.org/en/sponsor-
a-dog-or-cat/Default.aspx

You can make a regular monthly or one time donation to help the dogs and cats.

www.soidog.org/en/donate-today/Default.aspx

Donation of veterinary supplies – veterinarians often contact Soi Dog regarding the donation of much needed medicines and equipment.

www.soidog.org/en/donate-today/
donated-veterinary-supplies/

Consider making a legacy gift to Soi Dog in your Will. Check the Soi Dog website for information on Wills & Legacies Program.

www.soidog.org/en/wills-and-legacy-gifts/

You may wish to consider one of the above options as a gift to friends or family members. Soi Dog can send gift certificates to friends or family members as a personalized acknowledgement of your gift with a difference.

Your decision to help will be much appreciated, and help save the lives of the very animals you have read about in this book.

36

TRAVELING OVERSEAS? CAN YOU HELP A DOG OR CAT GET TO ITS NEW HOME?

Rescued dogs and cats need you to fly with them from Thailand.

For many of the cats and dogs at Soi Dog's shelter in Thailand, the only way they can travel to adopters overseas is as a passenger's extra baggage. Can you help by taking an animal back to your country when you return from your holiday?

They will take care of everything for you. A Soi Dog representative will bring the animal to the airport, meet you there prior to your flight and check the animal in. Upon arriving at your destination you will be met by the adopter. There is no work or expense on your part – it's simply standing near the Soi Dog representative while they sort everything out. Imagine the satisfaction you will feel when you see the animal first meet their new family.

© A flight volunteer helping to get an animal to its forever home.

If you are traveling on tickets booked with:

- Thai Airways
- Qatar
- Korean Air
- JAL
- EVA
- Lufthansa
- KLM
- Swiss Air
- Austrian Airlines

If you are interested in helping, please fill out the

online form.

www.soidog.org/en/be-a-flight-volunteer/
flight-volunteer-form/

Or contact jan@soidog-foundation.org for more information.

Even if you are not traveling from Thailand you can still help. You can donate your airline miles so a flight volunteer can help dogs and cats get to their new homes.

37

CONTACT DETAILS

TELEPHONE

Telephone (Phuket Shelter): (+66) 081 788 4222

Due to how busy they are, please check the Soi Dog website for the information you require before phoning, just in case someone is trying to phone through an emergency.

www.soidog.org/

Please note: The telephone is answered Monday to Friday from 8:00 am to 5:00 pm.

EMAIL

General Inquiries: info@soidog.org

Soi Dog Phuket Inquiries: info@soidog.org

Soi Dog Bangkok Inquiries: 093 0285 552 (mobile unit), BKKCentre@soidog-foundation.org

Adoptions: cristy@soidog.org

Donations: helen@soidog.org

Sponsorships of dogs: petra@soidog.org

Volunteering: volunteering@soidog-foundation.org

OVERSEAS OFFICES:

SDF Canada: candace@soidog-foundation.org

SDF Australia: belinda@soidog.org

SDF Switzerland/Germany: claudia@soidog.org

USA, UK, and Other Countries: romina@soidog.org

STREET & MAILING ADDRESS

Soi Dog Foundation
167/9 Moo 4
Soi Mai Khao 10
Tambon Mai Khao, Amphur Talang
Phuket 83110, Thailand

38

SOI DOG MERCHANDISE

There is a selection of Soi Dog products, where all the proceeds goes directly to the dogs and cats at the Soi Dog Foundation shelters.

www.soi-dog-foundation.myshopify.com/

CLOTHING

A selection of long-sleeve shirts, T-shirts, caps, hoodies, and singlets (muscle shirt).

GIFTS

Bandana, calendar, hand towel, keyring, silicone bracelet, pen, window card, and window sticker.

BAGS

Tote Bags, in an assortment of colours.

JEWELRY

A skinny bracelet, and a trio of bracelets.

VIRTUAL GIFTS - gifts for the cat and dog shelters

A selection to choose from. Ranging from animal treats, vaccines, toys, to puppy care packages.

39

WE ARE A REGISTERED CHARITY

Soi Dog is registered as a charity in six countries (so far).

Registration numbers are:
- Thailand: Phor.Gor. 39/2548
- USA: 27-1600444
- Australia: 58982568831
- Holland: 37120202
- France: W332011412
- UK: 1145142

(Pending charity registration in Canada and Switzerland).

Also, The Soi Dog Foundation are in association with:

40

THE SOI DOG STAFF PHOTOS

© Fundraising team and office staff.

© Adoptions team and office staff.

© The vet team.

© The co-founders John and Gill with the shelter staff and volunteers..

ABOUT THE AUTHORS

© Glen Johnson, September 2015.

Glen Johnson was born in England in 1973. He used to live in Devon, just a stones throw away from the English Riviera, but in August 2014, he gave away all his belongings, and bought a backpack, and he has been traveling Asia ever since. While he travels (with his older brother Gary), he will be helping charitable organizations, writing and releasing books about their foundations, leaving them with all the royalties (this book is the first of many). Glen is the author of forty-one fiction and non-fiction books, and is also on the development team for a new computer game called The Seed, from the creators of the award-winning S.T.A.L.K.E.R Misery mod. He has also started to release a collection of books about his travel adventures as they unfold, and Living the Dream: Part One – Khaosan Road, Thailand is available from all good ebook retailers. He loves to travel and has already visited thirty-five different countries, and lived in Mexico City, Mexico for far too long for a pale skinned European. He has also been married twice – and still refuses to say where he buried them.

Why not add Glen Johnson as a friend on Facebook, he is always happy to chat to likeminded people? From his author's page, you can keep up-to-date with all his new releases, and when his kindle books are free on Amazon. He checks it daily, so pop on and say hello! Don't be shy he's a friendly chap.

www.facebook.com/GlenJohnsonAuthor

Also, if you have a charity that would benefit from a free book, drop Glen an email. You never know, the next book he releases could be about your organization?

sinuousmindbooks@mail2bookmark.com

Alternatively, click 'Like' and you can follow Glen Johnson on Sinuous Mind Books official Facebook Page.

www.facebook.com/SinuousMindBooks

© Gary Johnson, May 2015.

Gary Johnson was born in England in 1972. He also used to live in the English Riviera, until his brother convinced him to travel around Asia with him. He has been living out of a backpack since August 2014, traveling extensively throughout five different countries. As well as co-authoring the Seven World Series, and the travel book, Living the Dream, he also co-owns Sinuous Mind Books, and Red Skull Publishing – online ebook and paperback companies that have released over a hundred books worldwide.

https://www.facebook.com/RedSkullPublishing

THANK YOU

From both myself, Gary, John, Gill, and everyone at the Soi Dog Foundation, we would like to thank you for buying the paperback version. Your purchase will make a physical difference to the stray dogs and cats of Thailand.

It's because of compassionate people like you that Soi Dog can continue caring for the animals in need – animals that have no voice. You give them a voice! You provide them with the food and care they need to live out the rest of their lives in peace and safety, and hopefully to be adopted into their Forever Homes.

© Puppy from the Puppy Run.

Printed in Great Britain
by Amazon.co.uk, Ltd.,
Marston Gate.